The Digital Library Survival Guide

By Joseph R. Matthews

Published by EOS International
2292 Faraday Avenue
Carlsbad, CA 92008
800-876-5484
www.eosintl.com

Matthews, Joseph R.
The Digital Library Survival Guide / Joseph R. Matthews
p. cm.
Includes bibliographical references and index.

1. Digital libraries. 2. Library materials – Digitization. 3. Archive materials – Digitization. 4. Electronic information resources. 5. Digital libraries – Collection development. I. Title.
Z692.C65 M 2011
025.00285

ISBN 978-0-9835874-0-8

Contents

Introduction

The purpose of any survival guide is to equip you with the necessary skills, tools and knowledge to survive and thrive in a specific environment or location. And this guide is no exception. The purpose of **The Digital Library Survival Guide** is to provide you with the tools you need so that you can begin to transition your library into the digital library of the future.

Among the tools that you would likely find of value were you suddenly transported to the wilds of Alaska or the remote plains of middle Australia are: a map, a compass, appropriate clothing, food (freeze dried if you don't want to carry a heavy pack), water, matches, and clothing appropriate for the locale. And a GPS might come in handy also. In addition to the tools, it would be helpful if you had some knowledge and experience about what is needed to survive, as well as having a clear idea of where you needed to travel in order to be rescued.

Hopefully, by the time you have completed reading this survival guide, not only will you know something about the tools needed to survive in our increasingly digital library environment, but you will understand something about the skills required to thrive in it.

I trust that you will find this survival guide to be of value and I wish you well on your journey.

Scot Cheatham

EOS International, CEO

Chapter 1

What's Happening Around Us

"Don't worry about what anybody else is going to do . . . The best way to predict the future is to invent it".

Alan Kay

You only have to step back a few paces and reflect on the amount of change that has occurred over the last twenty-five years in the mishmash and interaction of society and technology to be totally amazed – and bewildered. Among the more formidable challenges facing libraries today are tightened and/or declining budgets, rapid technological change, increased competition, customers who are technology-savvy, and calls for the library to demonstrate relevance and value. These challenges are forcing libraries to consider changing the ways they accomplish their traditional tasks as well as embracing new technologies in order to remain relevant to their customers.

Standing on the Shifting Sand of the Internet

Not surprising perhaps is that the largest challenge confronting any library is technology, specifically information technology. Over twenty years ago, a worldwide network – that wonderful thing called the Internet – was created where really large collections of digital resources in many different formats (text, video, audio, images and more) can be retrieved by anyone. Originally developed by scientists for use by other scientists worldwide, the scope of the Internet was expanded to allow anyone to become connected to the 'Net'. Digital information is stored on computers or servers connected to the Internet. Personal computers are used to gain access to the digital content. Increasingly, people expect that Internet resources are routinely made available to a broad array of mobile handheld devices so that access to information is "always on." In short, the **Internet changes everything**.

Libraries of all types have not been immune to the pressures of this relentless march towards pervasive digital content that is available on the Net. In order to facilitate access to this wealth of information resources for all, libraries have introduced public access computers, which provide access to the Internet. Libraries have added a variety of materials types such as MP3 players, DVDs, audio books, eBooks and so forth in an attempt to respond to customer demands. Many libraries have also installed wireless networks so that people can use their laptops and other devices to gain access to the Internet while they are in the library.

As the use of the Internet grew, it soon began to be recognized as a really disruptive force for old-line business and their traditional business models and a launch pad for new businesses. For example, Facebook has grown from a startup 7 years ago to a company with more than 600 million users and a private market value of over $30 billion – yep, that's Billion with a capital "B"! Similarly, Google was born about 10 years ago and has become the most popular search engine in the world

with a market valuation of more than $190 Billion –
there's that "B" word again.

Newspapers are getting wiped out in part because they
didn't realize they were in the information business—
they thought their business was about printing and
delivering papers. Newspapers are getting decimated
because the Internet has robbed them of their mini-
monopolies. For decades they had virtually no
competition, and so could charge ridiculous amounts of
money for things like tiny classified ads. Thanks to
Craigslist (and others), which came along and provided
the same service at no charge, the amount of revenue
loss to newspapers is simply staggering. Across the U.S.,
newspaper ad revenues are down more than $20 Billion
(TechCrunch 2009). The end result is that newspapers
are going out of business or are being trimmed so that
they are mere figments of their former robust selves.

Then again, consider that in 2003 the iPod/iTunes
combination was introduced and that it zoomed from
zero revenue to more than $10 billion in 2006 and up to
$12 billion in 2009. These numbers are really
staggering when you realize that each song sold online
at the iTunes Web site is only 99 cents.

Not surprisingly, the Internet continues to morph and
change. A decade or so ago, the ascent of the Web
browser as the center of the computing universe
appeared inevitable and indisputable. A recent Wired
magazine story "The Web Is Dead. Long Live the
Internet," illustrates the fact that a mere 23% of US
Internet traffic is Web-based and that this volume of
traffic is declining. What is increasing is mobile-based
traffic along with video downloads – by 51 percent.
Email and everything else barely registers (Anderson

2009). This article further reveals that really large sites, especially sites that are built on closed proprietary platforms (consider Facebook), are accounting for a disproportionate share of Internet traffic.

The 2010 Internet in Numbers[1]

Email

- 107 Trillion - Number of emails sent
- 294 Billion - Average number of emails per day
- 1.9 Billion - Number of email users worldwide
- 262 Billion - Number of spam emails per day (89%)

Web sites

- 255 million - number of Web sites (as of December 2010)
- 21.4 Million - number of new Web sites

Domain names (at the end of 2010)

- 202 Million - Total number of all domain names
- 88.8 Million - .com domain names
- 13.2 Million - .net domain names

The 2010 Internet in Numbers - continued

Social media (at the end of 2010)

- 600 Million - People on Facebook
- 250 Million - New people joining Facebook in 2010
- 30 Billion - Content (links, notes, photos and so forth) shared on Facebook each month
- 20 Million - Number of Facebook apps installed each day
- 25 Billion - Number of tweets sent on Twitter
- 175 Million - People on Twitter

Videos

- 2 Billion - Number of YouTube videos watched per day
- 35 - Hours of video uploaded to YouTube every minute
- 2+ Billion - Number of videos watched per month on Facebook
- 20 Million - Videos uploaded to Facebook per month

Images

- 5 Billion - Photos hosted by Flickr
- 3,000+ - Photos uploaded to Flickr per minute
- 3+ Billion - Photos uploaded to Facebook per month

[1]Data from Pingdom.com. Available at http://royal.pingdom.com/2011/01/12/internet-2010-in-numbers/

Rapid Technological Change

Even the most isolated of people would acknowledge that the speed with which technology continues to improve from a performance perspective is simply amazing. In 1965, Gordon Moore, a co-founder of Intel, observed this constant improvement in performance early in the development of computer chip technology. Moore's Law states that the number of transistors that are placed on an integrated circuit doubles approximately every two years. As a result the processing or performance capabilities of devices built from these integrated circuits or chips (computers, disk drives, digital cameras, cell phones and so forth) are similar to that of Moore's Law – a doubling in performance every two years. The end result for many people is that they have "techno lust" as evidenced by their desire to immediately purchase the latest and greatest.

While broadband access to homes and businesses in America is fairly high, the infrastructure being used has real limitations. Currently about 70 percent of homes have basic cable Internet provided by copper and coaxial cables that results in top speeds of about 5 megabits per second. Cable networks upgraded to fiber and coaxial cable (for the last few feet) can run at speeds in the hundreds of megabits per second. Want to learn about the speed of your network? – see the Internet Speed sidebar.

> **Internet Speed Testing**
>
> A quick search of the Internet will reveal a large
> number of sites that will test the speed of your
> Internet connection. For example, I used
> http://www.speedtest.net/
>
> The results showed that while the file download
> speed was 9.8 megabits per second (Mbs) the upload
> speed was crawling at .96 Mbs.

In 2009, the Federal Communications Commission
announced a National Broadband Plan that hoped to
deliver data speeds of 100 megabits per second (Mb/s)
to at least 100 million homes by 2020. Time will tell if
this objective can be achieved although in 2010 only
about 15 percent of homes have fiber optic cables
delivering Internet access (fiber can deliver speeds of
10,000 Mb/s or higher).

So the future is clearly going to be about faster, cheaper,
smaller devices with ever-increasing bandwidth. The
value of the Internet and the ever-growing number of
devices (and people) connected to it is known as
Metcalfe's Law that states:

> *"The usefulness or utility of a network
> equals the square of the number of users.
> In other words, the value of networked
> systems grows exponentially as the user
> population increases in a linear manner."*

Cloud computing

A broader concept is that of cloud computing which can be thought of as the ability to access remote computing resources via the Internet. Most frequently the "cloud" takes the form of Web-based tools or applications that users can access and use through a Web browser as if the application software was installed locally. The term "cloud" is used as a metaphor for the Internet (Han 2010). Cloud computing-based applications, whether fee-based or free, are generally expected to meet a minimum quality of service customer expectations and usually include a Service Level Agreement (SLA). Major cloud service providers include Amazon, Google and others. Amazon has launched a service called Simple Storage Solution that allows customers to store data for a few cents per gigabyte per month. Another service, Elastic Compute Cloud, lets a customer run software programs on Amazon's computers as if they were its own.

A major study completed by the Pew Research Center found that while cloud computing is confronting a number of problems (availability of broadband access, security, privacy, and quality of service) many survey respondents were comfortable suggesting that most people will be living 'mostly in the cloud' by 2020 (Anderson and Rainie 2010).

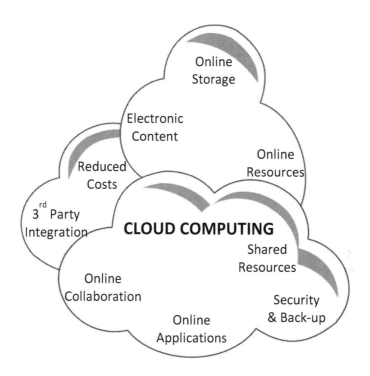

Nicholas Carr (2008) suggests that people will not even think about the location of the computer as cloud computing will be as commonplace as electricity. Sun Microsystems marketing slogan of the 1990s, "The Network is the Computer," begins to make sense in the era of cloud computing. Cloud computing can be divided into three categories: Software as a Service (SaaS), Platform as a Service (PaaS), and Infrastructure as a Service (IaaS).

Increasingly, software is being offered as a service or "Software as a Service" (SaaS). A provider licenses the software via the Internet using a "pay-as-you-go" model or as a free service. Many EOS customers have chosen the SaaS option.

The advantages of SaaS include:

- Save money by not having to purchase and maintain computer equipment, software licenses – no upfront capital costs
- Reduced staff costs to support the software
- Faster implementation
- Better software support – faster bug fixes
- Increased flexibility
- Automatic backups
- Improved security
- Built-in disaster recovery
- Accessible 24/7/365
- Improved customer satisfaction.

EOS International's Cloud-based Software-as-a-Service (SaaS) delivery option, EOS e-Library Service, offers an innovative, cost-effective alternative to the conventional in-house library automation system. Rather than installing software on a local server supported by in-house staff, your solution is hosted at the EOS Global Data Centers and supported directly by the same skilled technology and systems staff that develop it. Library staff and end-users access the software via a web browser over a secured Internet connection and experience the same functionality and appearance as if it were hosted locally.

PaaS focus on providing a hosted platform on which a specific software application can be deployed. Organizations can run a locally developed or a commercial software offering on a platform without having to worry about the operation of the computer hardware.

IaaS allows organizations to provision servers, storage space, and networking components to meet their computing needs. The IaaS organization is responsible for purchasing and installing the computer equipment, managing its network access and ensuring that the core components are operating efficiently and correctly, hardware, operating systems, Web server, firewall, and network connections.

The emergence of cloud computing has raised a significant issue. Once data exists in the cloud, who owns it? This is an issue that must be clearly addressed when a library is considering the use of cloud computing services.

For over 30 years, Electronic Online Systems (EOS) International has been developing, marketing and supporting award-winning library automation and knowledge management solutions for thousands of special libraries worldwide. EOS International is built on a solid foundation dedicated to achieving complete customer satisfaction.

Today, EOS is at the forefront of library automation and knowledge management, offering Web-based EOS.Web which provides anytime, anywhere connectivity to personalized information resources for employees, business partners and customers - whether they are across the hall or on the other side of the world. EOS is committed to protecting our clients' investment in time, resources and technology.

Mobile

The increased popularity of mobile computing is having a profound effect on the way people find, access, and process information. In short, the mantra of "I want it now!" is only growing louder and clearer. Over 70 percent of the world's population now has a mobile phone. That's over 5 billion mobile subscribers! In the U.S. and Europe it's 9 out of every 10 people that own a mobile device. Around the world many children are more likely to own a mobile phone than a book.

The popularity of the iPhone, iPad, and cell phones is simply staggering and will only grow. By the end of 2009, there were more than 250 million wireless data-capable devices in use in the United States (Vollmer 2010). A report by the Pew Research Center's Internet Project (2010) suggests that smart phones and other digital devices will soon replace personal computers (both desktops and laptops) as the primary means of access to information and communications. The individual is freed completely from wired sources. And these mobile devices will only get more powerful (thanks to Moore's Law) in the coming years. Thus, mobile is no longer an option; it has become a central behavior.

Mobile customers don't think of hardware, operating systems and communications technology yet they use them all seamlessly. The ubiquitous nature of mobile means that customers are changing the way in which they work and how they interact with others. In short, mobile users are always on in real-time connecting to other people and services since mobile is not a technology but rather is a behavior. Billions of people will access the Internet using a mobile device in 2011.

And in the U.S. more than 4 out of 5 households have mobile phones (and many have more than one mobile phone).

Applications designed to run on mobile devices are called apps or applets, popularized by Apple and its iPhone App store. The tens of thousands of available apps, some are free and some require payment of a small fee, are quite interesting and popular. There are over 330,000 apps available at the iPhone app store and over 200,000 apps for Androids. Apps are available to compare the price of an item (simply scan the barcode), pay bills and complete other bank-related actions, judge the beauty of someone, find reviews of a restaurant or business, store your airline boarding pass, track the progress and likely arrival time of an airline flight, determine the name of a star or constellation of stars at night, and ... well, the list goes on and on.

Some libraries have developed apps for use by their patrons. Some library specific apps include an online catalog, a map of the collection (the user clicks on the call number and the map shows where to find the item on the shelf), ask a reference question (via email or texting), and many more. Popular apps include people locators and collaboration tools that connect electronic information to objects in the physical world (Aldrich 2010). Apps have the potential intelligence to overcome content fragmentation of the Web and available information resources to deliver a simple yet powerful experience for the user. The world is changing as we move away from searching and move towards getting (through the use of an app).

Examples of Library Mobile Services

- Search online catalog
- Map of the location on the shelf of a desired item
- Place holds and loan-related services
- Map and directions to the library
- Hours open
- Links to mobile enabled databases
- Floor map
- Reserve a study room
- Library news
- Download podcasts, videos
- Download eBooks

Social networking

A social networking service is an online Internet service or Web site that facilitates interactions among people with similar interests and/or activities. Typically each user provides a profile of their interests and links to related information. Social networking sites allow individuals to share ideas, activities, events, and interests. Online community-based services are group-oriented. Facebook, Twitter, MySpace and LinkedIn are the most popular social networking sites in the US.

The Web is shifting from a paradigm of "publishing" to a model of "communication." It can be safely said that the majority of libraries have been slow to develop a presence on social networking sites and even when they do so, they have great difficulty finding their voice so that users find value in interacting with the library.

Technology Savvy Customers

People born between mid-1970s and the early 2000s, known as Generation Y or Millennials, are technologically savvy and now make up over 40% of the earth's population. These folks have no idea of life without cell phones, computers, digital music and the Internet. Gen Y individuals have little trust in authority and have very low attention spans. These Gen Y'ers have grown up accustomed to racial and religious integration, and more and more people are of mixed race or ethnicity. They expect to have multiple careers, know that they will encounter a great deal of change, and are generally comfortable with a fair amount of stress. Gen Y will look first to their peers for information and problem solving advice.

Gen Y'ers are increasingly sophisticated and are likely to manage their own data by setting up their own home networks, publish their own content, manage very large multimedia collections (iTunes, video and images), and really like to talk to one another. These folks are okay with lots of unedited, unvetted, unorganized stuff and like easy-to-learn services that provide immediate gratification. The principal question for libraries regarding the Gen Y population is how can the library become relevant in the lives of these individuals?

The available communication and information technologies are empowering the average person, students, scholars and others by making possible:

- Rapid and low-cost connection with others
- Tools that promote capacity for multi-tasking, multi-processing

- Connecting devices embedded in a wide variety of objects that are accessible and visible via the Internet
- Accessing an abundance of easily discovered recorded knowledge (Katz 2010).

Increased Competition

Clearly all types of libraries are under increasing pressure from both traditional and non-traditional competitors. Even individuals who consider themselves frequent library users are turning to other sources of information and entertainment for reasons of convenience. Among the more challenging competitors are online new and used bookstores such as Amazon.com, Half.com, Wikipedia, the huge number of Internet Web sites that turn up as a result of a Google search, and more.

Several authors have called for every library to re-invent itself using the perspective of the customer as the primary guide to implementing change by introducing new services and discontinuing services no longer valued by the customer (Matthews 2009).

Declining Budgets

As the recession of 2009 started to sink in to a wide variety of public and private organizations, the budgets of many libraries were reduced and then reduced again in 2010 (and more reductions are likely in 2011). This is particularly ironic for public libraries, as research has shown that use of the library increases in tough economic times. Many people are looking for help in assembling their resume, learning about job opportunities, applying for a job (many organizations will only accept online applications), as well as learning about ways to save money.

Growth of Digital Content

A project started in 1999 at the University of California Berkeley and now continued by the University of California San Diego tracks how much unique information is produced yearly. In 1999, the world produced between 1 and 2 exabytes of information or roughly 250 megabytes for every man, woman and child on earth. An exabyte is a billion gigabytes (a billion 1,000,000,000,000,000,000 bytes).

By 2002, print, film, magnetic and optical storage media produced about 5 exabytes of new information (Lyman & Varian 1999, Lyman & Varian 2002). It is difficult to comprehend exactly how big 5 exabytes of new information really is. Consider that five exabytes is roughly equivalent in size to the information contained in 500,000 new libraries the size of the Library of Congress print collections! This is about 800 megabytes of recorded information for each person in the world (about 6.3 billion people in 2002). Of all this new information, about 92 percent is stored on magnetic media, primarily hard disk drives.

Starting in 2008, rather than estimating the quantity of original content created each year, the project started estimating the amount of information that was consumed. The traditional media of radio and TV continues to dominate information consumption each day as more than three-quarters of US households information time is spent with non-computer sources. Yet, a full one-third of all words and more than half of all bytes are now received interactively - computers and hand-held digital devices (Bohn and Short, 2009).

Thus, the amount of digital content can only be expected to grow ever larger and larger making the discovery and use of information even more problematic for every one of us as individuals and as professional librarians.

Summary

The pace of change is unrelenting and seemingly accelerating year after year. The implications for libraries are serious and portend even more change as we move from the traditional library, to the transitional hybrid library, to a completely digital environment where all services in a digital library are delivered via the Internet.

However as we move to this "brave new library world," John Lombardi, president of the Louisiana State University System, offers a perspective that we should all reflect upon. Lombardi (2000) has offered *Lombardi's Rules for Digital Survival*:

- The objects are not as important as the content. Collection development becomes access development. Access to content is the primary mantra of all library work. Geography becomes increasingly irrelevant in a 24/7 digital world.
- Helping clients find resources in a digitally chaotic world is the first priority. Digitizing the rare book collection might be the second.
- If a vendor promises you seamless access and modular compatibility with any future developments, expect expensive upgrades.

- If others spend money on a similar project, let them finish before you start yours. Being first to invent large-scale digital library projects is for those with money to lose, tolerant customers, and tenure. If it will take ten years to deliver value, let someone else invest in it.
- If someone else has a service you need, buy it, do not invent it. If someone has 80% of the service you need, buy it; do not invent it.
- Nothing currently defining the Internet will remain recognizable after 5 years.
- There is safety in numbers; join consortia and urge others to take the lead.
- Invest in unique products only when you have a comparative advantage and someone else pays for it.
- For the next ten years, if it works well, is reliable, and you know how to use it, it is obsolete!

Survival Guide Tips

An important part of surviving is developing a clear understanding of the environment that is around you. This understanding will help guide you as you start a journey in which you not only survive but thrive!

- Recognize that change is occurring all around us and in many ways change is happening at an ever-increasing pace.
- The Internet changes everything.
- The amount of digital content is growing every year and people are expecting access to this mountain of digital content.
- Access is always on with hand-held mobile devices.
- Recognize that every library is facing real competition from every sector.
- Every library must take a fresh look at how it currently provides services and in partnership with its customers re-define the library in a digitally rich environment.

Chapter 2

The Evolving Library

"Today, however, the library is relinquishing its
place as the top source of inquiry. The reason that
the library is losing its supremacy in carrying out
this fundamental role is due, of course,
to the impact of digital technology.
As digital technology has pervaded
every aspect of our civilization, it has set
forth a revolution not only in how we store and
transmit recorded knowledge, historical records,
and a host of other kinds of communication but
also in how we seek and gain access to
these materials."

Jerry Campbell (2006)

A library is fundamentally a collection of various
materials usually kept in some kind of order such
as the Dewey Decimal system or the Library of
Congress classification system. Libraries are all about

gathering, organizing, using and (in some cases) preserving collections of materials. The end result is that the library has selected materials that are of high quality and that this quality is recognized and appreciated by the library's customers. With this reputation as the trusted source of reliable and high quality information, it is hoped that people will return again and again.

Typically the library creates a range of services that are designed to facilitate access to the library collections. These services might include reference services to answer customer questions, customer services desks, and programs.

The Classical Library

"There is the traditional citadel of manuscript and print, closed and guarded, a hierarchical structure as neatly ordered as a vast set of display cabinets for butterflies. Its expert librarians pin every document, book, and journal in the collection to its proper place, the precise category in which equally expert researchers will be sure to find it."

Anthony Grafton (2009)

The classical or traditional library is an artifact-bound institution that deals with tangible objects that are owned by the library (Lewis 1998). People visit the library to use the objects in the physical library or the items are borrowed for a period of time. Local collections of materials have been required to provide convenient neighborhood access to the physical containers of information – books, magazines, CDs and so forth.

Some libraries, especially academic libraries, have focused on providing access to a wide variety of materials. This has meant acquiring larger and larger numbers of books "just-in-case" the item was of possible interest at some point in the future. Thus, these large libraries spent sizable amounts of money constructing very large buildings to house these ever-increasing collections. Some have called these large buildings 'warehouses' storing collections of dead-trees. For some large research libraries size mattered to such an extent that the library building was almost viewed as a 'cathedral.'

Most of the objects in a library are information resources of some kind. The objects are selected using a collection development policy or criteria that typically include measures of quality. The information resources are organized – cataloged, classified and indexed by human beings in a carefully controlled process. These bibliographic and authority records act as surrogates to the physical information resources in the discovery process using the library's online catalog. Searches can be conducted using specific combinations of fields or subfields or the contents of the entire record may be searched.

Libraries also developed a series of tools, for example, the library catalog, to assist the customer in finding items of interest. And, over time, libraries introduced reference services to help customers cope with the increasing complexity of finding tools – different index tools for different areas of a collection, e.g., science, medicine, general literature, newspapers and so forth.

As Evans & Wurster (1997) explain, to the extent that information is embedded in physical modes of delivery (consider a book as a physical mode of delivery), a trade-off exists between richness and reach.

- *Richness*, which has three components: the amount of information conveyed (bandwidth), the amount of customization available for the delivery of information; and its level of interactivity.
- *Reach* is the number of people who can receive the information. In general, the reach of the traditional library is limited by people's willingness to invest time and energy to get to the physical library.

The value of a library to its user has historically revolved around two concepts: the library collected high quality materials (the "good stuff"), and the good stuff was free to use. However, access to information resources was by necessity on-site. The physicality of the library created a sense of place and an immersion into a wealth of information resources.

Admittedly the customer did experience some actual out-of-pocket expenses having to travel to the library and learning to navigate within the library to find the desired materials. The fact that libraries are central to many organizations and communities is attested to by their continuing use and the growth of that use.

Organizations and communities fund the library because it is recognized that the library creates public good. Libraries make information more available to individuals than would be the case if individuals were left on their own. The end result is that the organization is more productive and it also enhances the quality of life in communities.

Libraries have developed a series of processes to ensure that the collection is refreshed on a regular and periodic basis, that the materials remain organized, that customers can access the materials of interest, that they can borrow these materials, and that the library will ensure that the materials are returned so that others may use the items again and again.

The traditional library is, in fact, an artifact-based organization that houses a collection of materials that contain information. However, information is being freed from their containers or artifacts and thus the artifacts are losing their centrality.

The real problem is that the value of library collections is rooted in the worth of a local copy. The localness of something loses most of its embodied value when you can retrieve information from anywhere in milliseconds. The notion of a copy loses most of its embodied value when there's no longer a difference between transmission and duplication. When dealing with digital objects, to transmit it is to duplicate it. If an individual downloads a copy, the original still remains and can be accessed again and again. Thus, the local copy stops being so important.

The Digital Library

> *"There's an illusion being created that all of the world's knowledge is on the Web, but we haven't begun to glimpse what is out there in local archives and libraries. Material that is not digitized risks being neglected, as it would not have been in the past, virtually lost to the great majority of potential users."*
>
> Katie Hafner (2007)

The term 'digital library' has been used for a considerable period of time and while its meaning has been defined in some cases, more often than not, its meaning has been assumed. A digital library has been variously called the virtual library, the electronic library, the library of the future, and the library without walls (Bawden & Rowlands 1999). Further, the use of the phrase "digital library" obscures the complex relationship between electronic information collections and the library as an institution (Borgman 1999).

J.C.R. Licklider (1965) is his book *Libraries of the Future* reported on a two-year project that explored the topic of "assembling information in recorded (digital) form and of organizing and making it available for use." The project team defined the scope of the project as:

> *"functions, classes of information, and domains of knowledge in which the items of basic interest are not the print or paper, and are not the words and*

sentences themselves – but the facts, concepts, principles, and ideas that lie behind the visible and tangible aspects of documents."

Such a scope of work is considerably broader than many today would imagine that the concept of a 'digital library' would encompass. The Association of Research Libraries synthesized several definitions of the "digital library" and suggested that the common elements include:

- The digital library is not a single entity;
- The digital library requires technology to link the resources of many;
- The linkages between the many digital libraries and information services are transparent to the end users;
- Universal access to digital libraries and information services is a goal; and
- Digital library collections are not limited to document surrogates: they extend to digital artifacts that cannot be represented or distributed in printed formats.

The US Digital Library Federation (now a part of the Council on Library and Information Resources), has produced the following definition:

"Digital libraries are organizations that provide resources, including specialized staff, to select, structure, offer intellectual access to, interpret, distribute, preserve the integrity of, and ensure the persistence over time of collections of digital works so that they are readily and economically

available for use by a defined community or set of communities." (DLF, 1998).

For our purposes, the **digital library** is defined as:

A collection of digital content that uses information technologies to acquire, store, manage, conserve and provide access to a broad spectrum of digital information.

Thus, we can consider a digital library has:

- A *collection* of digital objects in a wide variety of formats
- *Information* about the objects (metadata)
- Appropriate *services* (search, browse, save, email, annotate, share ...)
- *Online* delivery of services and content.

Perhaps the most important distinction of a digital library is that all of the objects in the digital library – text, sounds (audio), video, images and everything else – have the potential for being treated in essentially the same way. And since what is delivered to the customer is a **copy**, which is not returned to the library after use, many of the traditional processes used by a library to track the borrowing of materials are no longer necessary.

The logical conclusion is that the concept of a library's collection and the library itself as a place-based institution no longer holds true, since the digital library can deliver services anytime, anywhere. Thus, a customer will not need to visit the physical library but rather can visit the virtual or digital library when it is convenient. Most, if not all, libraries will progress steadily to a fully digital state over time. Implementation of the digital library will require significant organizational change and require librarians to develop new competencies.

Given this reality, it is not surprising that some have articulated a fundamental question – "why do we need libraries?" The answer to this question is answered indirectly in the following chapters and directly in the final, concluding chapter.

The term 'virtual library' or 'electronic library' is often used interchangeably with that of the 'digital library.' More often than not the use of the term 'virtual library' seems to emphasize that a digital library need not be restricted to a single collection of digital materials but rather focuses on the ability to "collect" information across a large number of distributed sites on the network.

It is possible to consider a digital library from alternative conceptual viewpoints. For example, Christine Borgman (1999) has suggested three possible views of the digital library:

- As content, collections and communications
- As institutions or services
- As databases.

Perhaps a better understanding of what constitutes a digital library is provided by Rowlands and Bawden (1999) who suggest that a digital library is composed of three domains:

Social domain

- Human factors involved in accessing, evaluating and using information. Libraries have historically focused on providing access to high-quality materials (the 'good stuff') but in the age of Google the library is often the "court of last resort" when it comes to finding information. The pervasive impact of Google is illustrated by the phrase "did you Google it?" Two major studies by OCLC (2003 and 2005) highlighted the fact that libraries are not the top choice for access to electronic resources. It is important to remember that convenience (fast, free, and that almost always means Google) will always trump quality (of a library's collections).

- Organizational factors that may be necessary to accommodate the changes in staffing skills, staffing mix, workflow of processes that will be required to provide customers with a digital library.

- Library management factors that will result when the digital library is introduced in a traditional library or a 'digital' only digital library are created. For example, a flatter organizational structure may be best, especially with staff geographically dispersed (after all, no need to come to work at the 'digital library').

- Information law and policy factors may be considerable in the development of a digital library - for example, the availability of back issues of journals, copyright for published materials, intellectual ownership of materials donated to the library, document authenticity, information integrity, and so forth.

- Impacts on the information transfer chain become clear when it is recognized that the same digital material (a journal article for example) may be available from many different locations on the Internet.

Information domain

- Knowledge organization and discovery (e.g., metadata) become very important in the virtual arena as the customer does not have the opportunity of interacting with a library staff member face-to-face should a problem arise. In addition, discovering the availability of various types of digital content - that is, text, audio, video, images – raises a number of interesting technical issues that must be solved within the context of an easy to use online user interface.
- Impacts on the information transfer chain (e.g., supply) become problematical since the library is no longer purchasing digital content but rather is licensing it (renting it). What assurances does a library have that the supplier will be around in 10, 25 or more years to ensure that the library's customers will have access?

Systems domain

- Human factors (e.g., human-system interaction) become increasingly important in an environment as complex as that of the digital library. What will the user interface of a search (or discovery as it is sometimes called) system look like in order to handle request for images, video, audio or textual information? The solution must involve close interaction with system developers and actual users to develop a user interface that is not cumbersome or difficult to use.

- System factors that are present to enable the interchange of information from one system to another to facilitate the finding of useful information. In addition to interoperability another challenge revolves around the scalability of the system to handle the exponentially increasing amount of digital content.

- Knowledge organization and discovery (e.g., software agents) become even more important as people move from desktop access to the Internet to the use of a wide range of hand-held devices (cell phones, PDAs and other devices). Discovery of information in a mobile setting will require use of "apps" that can be quickly downloaded and will have real value to the library's customers.

- Impacts on the information transfer chain (technical) which requires the library to authenticate the valid use of an electronic resource when a connection is made from one system to another.

The digital library may be based on an existing institution or it may focus on a subject discipline, a vocation or profession, a region or a nation. Among the distinguishing features of a digital library are:

- *Open Access*: Powerful search and browse capabilities facilitate the discovery of information and digital resources.

- *Wide Variety of Information*: Any object that can be digitized can be included in a digital library – text, images, audio, video and more.
- *Sharing of Information*: Digital libraries embrace the traditional library concept of sharing resources. The sharing of digital information can occur more rapidly than the movement of a physical object.
- *Ubiquitous Access*: Anyone can access the digital content provided they have access to a computer or digital device that is connected to a communications network. And access can occur at any time – 24 hours a day, 7 days a week (Fox & Urs, 2002).
- *Multiple Access*: Many individuals can use the same resource simultaneously.
- *Improved Preservation and Conservation.* While digitization is not a long-term preservation solution for physical collections, it does provide access to materials that are, in many cases, disintegrating due to acid in paper or improper storage of the materials.
- *Added Value.* Some digital content, e.g., images, can be enhanced using digital technology. In addition, the users of the digital library can add value by tagging the digital content. Some libraries have been pleasantly surprised to discover that users are identifying specific individuals found in photographs accessible via the digital library.

In 1996, the National Science Foundation announced the Digital Library Initiative (DLI) and subsequently funded a number of large research projects. The Initiative's focus was to dramatically advance the means to collect, store, and organize information in digital forms, and make it available for searching, retrieval, and processing via communication networks -- all in user-friendly ways. The six US-based organizations that received funding under this Initiative included:

- The University of California at Berkeley – Environmental planning and geographic information systems (GIS)
- The University of California at Santa Barbara – Spatially-referenced map information (The Alexandria Project)
- Carnegie-Mellon University – Infomedia digital video library
- University of Illinois at Urbana-Champaign – Federating repositories of scientific information
- University of Michigan – Intelligent agents for information location
- Stanford University – Interoperation mechanisms among heterogeneous services (Liew 2009).

All of these projects published a variety of research reports and journal articles, some of which are cited in this book. The National Science Foundation has also sponsored a number of Web sites related to science, engineering and teaching – see the National Science Digital Library (NSDL) portal sidebar.

National Science Digital Library (NSDL) Portals

Biology	biosciednet.org
Chemistry	jchemed.chem.wisc.edu
Computational science	shodor.org/refdesk
Engineering	engineeringpathway.com/ep/
Materials science	matdl.org
Mathematics	mathdl.maa.org
Physics & astronomy	compadre.org
Social science	qssdl.org
Community colleges	amser.org
Informal science	howtosmile.org
Middle school	msteacher.org
Teachers	teacherdomain.org

As Constance Malpas has noted, "We've built up infrastructures that are all bound up in print materials. The sheer physicality of our collections has led us to come up with resource and staffing models that are not a good fit for our digital environment. That's what is liberating and a little scary about founding a new [digital] library" (Henry 2010).

Thus, an all-digital library provides online access to its collections of journals, reference works, digitized books, and other digital materials. To serve the needs of the library's customers, there must first be a critical mass of quality materials available electronically. Most libraries will find that the number of eJournals available online greatly exceeds the library's ability to pay for all that digital content. Interestingly, an analysis prepared by the OCLC Research staff found that 30 percent or more of a library's local book collection was already present in digital form and that this was likely to grow to 50 percent over the next 3 years (Malpas 2010). This is a direct result of the Google Books project!

Tip!

Check out this Web site

for a comprehensive list

of digital libraries!

http://www.academicinfo.net/digital.html

The future all-digital library is interesting to contemplate. Daniel Greenstein, vice provost for Academic Planning, Programs and Coordination in the Office of the President at the University of California has suggested that the all-digital library would have a small staff, have a small physical footprint focused on special collections, and outsource many of its operations (Kolowich 2009).

The realization that one cannot simply store digital data away once and forget about it, simply trusting that the data will be intact and retrievable years later, may strike some as trite but recognition of this fact has significant operational implications for the digital library in the years to come.

Critical to the development of an all-digital library is the re-invention of the library's traditional mission in a digital context, so that the library focuses on helping people find, manage, and use information. The library will need to combine information and communication technologies together with a range of library services that bring people together building communities rather than reinforcing their digital isolation. In short, the library must understand how it adds value in the life of the customer.

William Arms (1995) suggested that there are eight general principles that should be followed when creating a digital library:

- The technical framework for the library exists within a legal and social framework
- Understanding of digital library concepts is hampered by terminology
- The underlying architecture should be separate from the content stored in the library
- Names and identifiers are the basic building block for the digital library
- Digital library objects are more than collections of bits
- The digital library object that is used is different from the stored object
- Repositories must look after the information they hold
- Users want intellectual works, not digital objects.

The value of utility of a digital library can be better understood if the relationships between the user, the system, and the content are clearly defined as shown in Figure 2-1. Discoverability and the manipulation of digital objects is becoming more important than in an age of collaboration, sharing, media manipulation and interaction in a social network-centric world.

Figure 2-1. Components of the Digital Library*

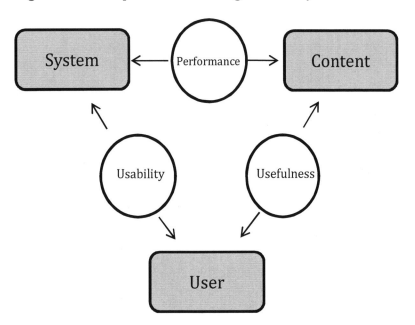

*Adapted from Tsakonas and Papatheodorou 2008.

The Hybrid Library

> *"Real libraries do not split neatly into*
> *reactionary temples of leather and vellum and*
> *hip, accessible banks of humming computers -*
> *though many journalists, even a few librarians,*
> *write and speak as if they did."*
>
> Anthony Grafton (2009)

The term 'hybrid library' is often used to describe the reality facing almost all libraries today. That is the working library must provide access to and provide processes to support collections in both electronic and print environments. The library continues to provide services in a physical location to a range of collections that come in a wide-array of materials types – books, magazines, CDs, video DVDs, eBooks, microforms (in some cases) – as well as supporting access to electronic resources (eJournals, collections of eJournals, and other related database products). Given the popularity of 'words' that contain an 'e' as the first character – eBooks, eBook readers, eJournals – some have started to use the term 'pBook' for the traditional printed book!

For many, the hybrid library is viewed as a transitional stage towards an all-digital library. The challenge confronting every library today is how fast does the hybrid library move to become a total 'digital library' (with no physical presence that someone can visit) or will it always be a hybrid library? The range of options for libraries is shown in Figure 2-2 that emphasizes relative degrees of distributed access and digital content. For others, the hybrid library represents the final destination with the library providing access to information from a variety of media and formats.

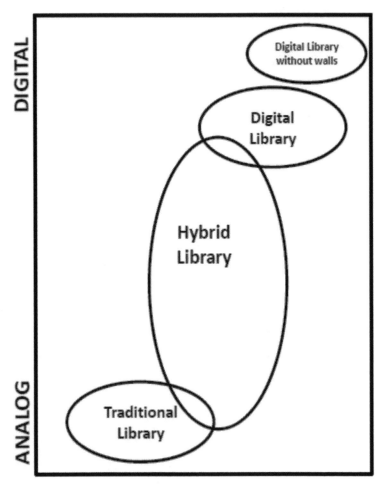

Figure 2-2 Library Concepts

Since the hybrid library embraces a physical location where materials are stored and made accessible, it preserves the notion of the traditional library. Some librarians may focus new attention on the library as 'place' while others may see the hybrid library as a gateway library (with place having a role (or should that be 'place' having a place?). While pBooks, print journals, DVDs, CDs exist within the library, they are being overshadowed by digital resources which are accessible 24/7. If an item is not available online, it has less and less importance to many library users. The treasures of a library's collection will not be unearthed unless those materials are available online.

Clearly one of the challenges of managing a real-world hybrid library is that old and new technologies must co-exist within a coherent set of services. And any cost savings that may accrue as the result of moving towards the digital environment may not be realized unless the library eliminates the print copies of journals and books. Many libraries are seeing their print materials budget reduced as more of the acquisitions budget is going to the licensing of electronic resources.

"We don't know where it's going or how it will end up.

Anyone who thinks they do is just fooling themselves.

There is instability in the environment.

Everyone used to know what a library was.

But there are no agreed-upon parameters

for this digital onslaught."

John Lombardi

The hybrid library must be compelling in order to retain existing customers and to attract new customers – in both the physical and digital library environments.

EOS.Web Digital

Digital & Hybrid Libraries

See Chapter 11, Digital Library Best Practices, for more information on EOS.Web Digital.

Summary

Clearly the fundamental mission of libraries – to facilitate access to knowledge and information – has remained unchanged, while the processes, tools and systems used have undergone fundamental transformation. These fundamental changes can be summarized as shown in Table 2-1 (Fox and Urs, 2002).

The hybrid and digital libraries offer access to a wider range of digital materials (sometimes called digital objects) that must be accessible in multiple venues, which allows the end-user to discover resources using a variety of means. A digital library is not a replacement for the traditional library but rather represents the future of traditional libraries.

The near elimination of distance or the need for physical locations to house collections and the use of computer and communications infrastructure give rise to countless new possibilities for redefining and exploring what the digital library of the future will become. Libraries need to focus on the ways its customers communicate, share, search, and repurpose information if they are to be effective and bring value in the life of their customers.

Table 2-1

Traditional Libraries	Digital Libraries
Stable environments with change evolving slowly.	Highly dynamic environments as evidenced by many versions of the 'same' digital object.
Content is primarily print, usually well-defined and categorized and rarely linked to one-another.	Digital objects are multimedia, and vary in size and quality. Multiple links can be created between digital objects.
Objects are located in a physical space.	Objects are not located in a physical or logical place.
Organization and structuring of content is flat. Bibliographic records describing content are tightly controlled.	Non-hierarchical relationships exist among and between digital objects. Descriptive metadata can be very rich and are not controlled.
Collections and the library catalog are separate entities.	Data and metadata converge into a single medium.
Library collections are organized.	Digital objects do not need to be organized.
Content is scholarly in nature and selection is a careful controlled process.	Content is not limited to scholarly content.

Table 2-1 – continued.

Traditional libraries	Digital libraries
Limited access points and the catalog reflects a 'library' orientation.	Extensive access points with distributed collections, control and content management is possible.
The physical and logical organization is tightly controlled.	Collections may be virtual as the physical and logical organization can be separated.
One way (read-only) interactions and processes.	Two-way and richer interactions possible as people communicate remotely, interactively and informally.
Users of the library (and library catalog) well-studied and generally understood.	Users' individual differences and seeking behaviors not well studied.
The culture supports free and universal access.	Free and as well as fee-based access to digital content.
Library Web site is a megaphone – here we are.	The Web is a fundamentally new way of getting work done.

Survival Guide Tips

Being aware of the weather in a survival situation is only good common sense. Most importantly, you should be aware of when and how the weather is likely to change. Will the temperature drop significantly? Is rain, sleet or snow likely to come in the next hour or day? Knowing the answers will help you decide whether you should take immediate shelter or if you have time to move to your intended destination.

- Is your organization a classical library, a completely digital library or a hybrid?
- Does your library have unique materials that your customers would like to access online?
- Recognize that the value of the physical collection's local copy diminishes in a digital environment.
- Learning more about your library customer's use of information in their day-to-day lives is crucial in gaining an understanding of how your library needs to change.
- While providing access to digital content is important it is much more important to provide a user interface that provides context so that the user is better able to understand and use the content.
- Recognize that the hybrid library is a bifurcated library that needs to provide traditional services while moving (how far is the question?) to provide digital library services. Thus, the library's budget is likely to increase during this transition.

Chapter 3

Digitization

"No matter what the industry,
or if the consumers of digital and media assets
are internal or external to an organization,
there are ever increasing expectations
that content will be available
anytime, anywhere and on any device."

Henry Stewart

D igitization is a set of processes of converting physical resources into digital form. Implicit in the digitization process is the need to describe these digitized materials in a meaningful way (this process produces descriptive metadata) so that the digital material can be retrieved and used. Given the high costs associated with digitization, it is important to recognize and treat the digitized materials as 'digital assets'.

While publishers of magazines and academic journals in the 1990s could foresee a future in which all of their published content was accessible as digital content on the Web, book publishers were less inclined to embrace such a vision. Then, in late 2004, Google announced their partnership with the libraries of Harvard, Stanford, the University of Michigan, the University of Oxford, and the New York Public Library to digitally scan books from their collections so that users worldwide would have access to the full-text of their collections.

Mass Digitization Projects

The Google announcement that it had signed partnership agreements with five large major research libraries to digitize their book collections touched off a frenzy of excitement and activity. An analysis of the five original library holdings revealed that more than 60 percent of the aggregate print book collection consists of books held by a single library. Thus the collection overlap (a book held by two or more libraries) is less than 40 percent, which was a bit of a surprise (Lavoie et al 2005).

Since then more than twenty-seven national, university and public libraries have joined the project and are having their book collections digitized (Google Books nd). This collaboration between Google and the libraries has been called "Googlebrary" (Maxymuk 2005).

Google decided to digitize all of the books in a library's collection – in the public domain (out of copyright) and in copyright (and most likely out-of-print). Google makes full-text versions available if the book is in the public domain (out of copyright) and only shows snippets or brief excerpts if they are still under copyright protection. Thus, the resulting debate between Google and publishers, authors, libraries and others has often been acrimonious. Interestingly, Google invoked the fair use doctrine (this doctrine provides a limitation or exception to the exclusive right of copyright. Examples of fair use include commentary, criticism, news reporting, research, teaching, library archiving and scholarship), which many found to be ironic and unacceptable with the end result that several parties have sued Google. A proposed settlement was announced in October 2008 and a revised settlement proposed in October 2009. Finally, on March 22, 2011 the Court denied the parties' request for final settlement approval. The parties are considering their next steps.

Google Books uses high-speed scanners, the size of a small SUV, with automatic page-turners to digitize each book at the rate of 1,000 pages per hour. The image is saved as one file (with a resolution of either 200 dpi or 300 dpi) and the images are then converted to text using optical character recognition software. The resulting text file is saved as a file and linked to the image file. Google has had to learn a great deal about making searching for books efficient and effective since it can't rely on *PageRank* – its proprietary tool that ranks Web sites based on the number of links from other Web sites to a particular Web page for its search engine. Google uses more than 100 "signals" or characteristics about the book that it integrates in an algorithm to rank the search results when using Google Books (Madrigal 2010).

In order to ensure access to their digitized collections, the US-based libraries participating in the Google book-scanning project are creating a joint platform to store, preserve and ultimately access their copies of the Google digital versions of their collections. The platform is run by the University of Michigan and called the Hathi Trust.

Clearly, a lot of money will be made from digitizing books – when content moves from the physical to digital, its value jumps significantly. A copy can be "sold" fairly easily in the online environment many times. The goal from Google's perspective is to provide access to the content of Google Books. And, it is true, the digitization of the library collections is a good form of insurance for providing access, especially for the many books that are deteriorating from age, neglect or were printed on acid-based paper (which disintegrates over time).

> *"For a growing (but not universal)*
>
> *portion of the Web and the world,*
>
> *we allow Google to determine*
>
> *what is important, relevant, and true."*
>
> Siva Vaidhyanathan (2010)

It is also interesting to note that projects like Google Books fundamentally change the library profession's understanding of how a library adds value for its customers. Library collections are not a random bunch of stuff but rather are the result of a consciously created, carefully selected, deliberately maintained, assembly of materials. Now with the advent of a very large collection of digitized books, a fundamental question must be addressed: How is a library to straddle the two realities facing them – providing access to and maintaining an analog collection as well as providing access to and maintaining a large digitized collection of materials? For most libraries, this is a question that is being addressed on a day-by-day basis as there is no clear path as to what lies ahead.

Copyright

Copyright bestows upon the creator of a work a temporary monopoly – originally 14 years in the United States – over any copies of the work. The idea was to encourage artists and authors to create even more works that could be shared with others through the use of copies. This meant then that after the 14-year period others could freely use the work as it was in the public domain or commons.

Since the original 1976 copyright law, Congress has made revisions and extended the copyright period so that today, after almost constant tweaking and nudging, the copyright expiration data is now an additional 70 years beyond the life span of the creator (Congress responded to commercial copyright holders such as Disney who wanted to protect their monopoly over their various characters and movies). Thus anything created today will not return to the commons until the next century.

In the world of books this has had a perverse effect. About 15 percent of the older books are in the public domain; 10 percent of books are still in print; while publishers have abandoned 75 percent of books. These abandoned books are sometimes referred to as "orphans." The publisher does not find it profitable to keep these books in print and in some cases, who actually owns the copyright is unclear - the publisher or the author? As a result of the Google book-scanning project (where everything is scanned – regardless of copyright), the legal limbo surrounding the status of these orphans has caused much consternation and the legal bills continue to mount. The real argument that is occurring is a clash in business models as technology has enabled the sharing of digital copies for little or no cost. Digital technology has disrupted all business models based on mass-produced copies (newspapers, magazines, books and so forth). In the digital environment, copies freely flow everywhere (whether desired or not). Thus, copies lose value (Kelly 2006).

Google Books is providing four possible book views:

- *Full views* where Google has permission to "publish" the entire book as well as for books out of copyright (books published prior to 1923)
- *Limited view*, which includes a few preview pages from the book that can be browsed
- *Snippet view*, where one can search a book and find up to three snippets of information for each search, and
- *No preview option* that provides information about the book and links of where to find or buy the book.

Of interest to libraries is that a user who finds an item through Google Books can link directly to the online catalog of the closest library that has the item in their library catalog (OCLC shares their *WorldCat* catalog with Google).

The proposed settlement would allow every library to be able to search Google Books using one computer at no charge. Should the library want to provide more than one computer to access Google Books then the library would need to pay Google for this option. It is kind of ironic that libraries will need to pay Google to gain access to the digital version of books those libraries paid for previously (admittedly Google has spent a lot of money in the process of digitizing the various library book collections).

In essence libraries would end up paying subscription fees for access to some digitized material they now own in print. In addition, the settlement would create a Book Rights Registry that would pay authors a small fee when a copy of their book was purchased and downloaded (provided the author agreed to participation in the Book Rights Registry.

Recently, Eric Hellman, who created the concept of the OpenURL (a special type of URL that carries bibliographic information), proposed a new model for the 70 percent of orphaned books. Eric's new creation, GlueJar, would allow a publisher to identify books they want to "unglue." The publisher sets a price and people contribute money (think, micro donations) towards the ungluing. When the threshold is reached the digital book would appear in a wide number of repositories and would be available to anyone under the Creative Commons license. Interesting idea.

Other Mass Digitization Projects

Million Book Project, also known as the Universal Library, was created to foster creativity and free access to all human knowledge. As a first step in realizing this mission, the Million Book Project has created a free-to-read, searchable collection of one million books, available to everyone over the Internet. While most of the books were scanned in India, many libraries from around the world are adding scanned works to this collection.

How Big Is a Million Books?

The prospect of digitizing and providing access to a million books is clearly a huge task. Consider:

If the average book is 1 inch thick, 1 million books stacked on top of one another would reach 83,333 feet tall (or 15.78 miles in height or 3 times the altitude of typical airplane flight across the country)

Assuming the average book is 12 inches high, 1 million books laid end-to-end would be about 146 miles

If the average book weighs 1.5 pounds, then 1 million books would weigh about 750 tons

If the average book contains about 350 pages, then the 1 million books would have slightly more than 350 million pages of text

The 1 million books would contain about 70 billion words

The disk space required to store all of the text from 1 million books would be about 43,000 gigabytes.

Internet Archive is a non-profit organization that was founded to build an Internet library. Its purposes include offering permanent access for researchers, historians, scholars, people with disabilities, and the general public to historical collections that exist in digital format. The Internet Archive is working to prevent the Internet - a new medium with major historical significance - and other "born-digital" materials from disappearing into the past.

In 2006, Microsoft started a book-scanning project, called **Live Search Books**, and subsequently stopped scanning books in 2008. All of the 750,000 scanned book data as well as 80 million journal articles created as part of this Microsoft project were subsequently given to the Internet Archive.

The Internet Archive and Yahoo conceived the **Open Content Alliance** (OCA) in 2005 as a way to offer free broad, public access to a rich panorama of digital resources. Metadata for all content is freely exposed to the public using the Open Archives Initiative Protocol for Metadata Harvesting (OAI-PMH) and RSS. More than 1 million digital books are accessible using the OCA Web site. More than 100 academic research libraries are contributing digital content to the Open Content Alliance – libraries that join the OCA must pay to have their content scanned or do it themselves.

The Digital Public Library of America

Recently, Harvard University Chief Librarian Robert Darnton issued a challenge to create a Digital Public Library of America, sometimes called the National Digital Library. Darnton organized a group of representatives from foundations, cultural institutions, libraries and scholarly organizations to assemble the collections of US archives, museums, and universities (Zax 2010). Darnton has suggested that there are a host of political, financial, technological, and legal challenges that must be addressed and solved. The digital library envisioned by this group would be an open, distributed network of comprehensive online resources drawn from the countries public libraries, archives, museums, and universities.

The Digital Public Library of America is not a utopian dream but can be achieved because:

- The technology exists to digitize the holdings of very large libraries as demonstrated by Google's book scanning project
- A coalition of libraries could be formed to share their collections for digitization
- A coalition of foundations and other nonprofit organizations could be formed to cover the costs
- A central organization could be created to deal with problems of coordination, processing, and preservation.

The World Digital Library

The World Digital Library (WDL – www.wdl.com) makes available on the Internet, free of charge and in multilingual format, significant primary materials from countries and cultures from around the world. The content is in a variety of formats and languages, from different places and time periods. While the content is not translated, the metadata describing the content is translated into seven languages – Arabic, Chinese, English, French, Russian, and Spanish (the official languages of the United Nations) - so that users can search and browse the content in multiple languages. In addition to multilingual access, the World Digital Library has the following functionality:

- Consistent metadata – every item is cataloged by place, time, topic, format of item and contributing institution
- Item-level descriptions – a paragraph length description explains what the item is and why it is important

- Enhanced view and zoom features – the user can navigate in order to see more details of the item
- Curator videos – selected items feature videos that provide in-depth explanations about the item or group of items.

The vast majority of the content to be found in the WDL is being contributed by the national libraries from countries from around the world. In addition, other academic and special libraries have joined the World Digital Library project. The US Library of Congress maintains the WDL Web site.

National Digital Libraries

Almost every country's national library has created a digital library where photographs, audio and video files, as well as full-text from books and other cultural documents are made accessible to the user. For example, France has announced that it will spend 750 million Euros to digitize the French cultural patrimony. The National Library of the Netherlands aims to digitize within ten years every Dutch book, newspaper and periodical produced from 1470 to the present. The national libraries of Japan, Norway, Finland and Australia have announced similar programs.

58

Country	Web site
Argentina	http://www.bn.gov.ar/
Australia	http://www.pictureaustralia.org/index.html
Austria	http://www.onb.ac.at/index.php
Belgium	http://www.kbr.be/accueil_fr.html
Brazil	http://www.bn.br/portal/
Canada	http://www.banq.qc.ca/accueil/
Chile	http://www.dibam.cl/biblioteca_nacional/
China, People's	http://www.nlc.gov.cn/
China, Republic	http://www.ncl.edu.tw/mp.asp?mp=5
Czech Republic	http://www.nkp.cz/
Denmark	http://www.kb.dk/da/index.html
Egypt	http://www.darelkotob.gov.eg/
Finland	http://www.kansalliskirjasto.fi/
France	http://www.bnf.fr/fr/acc/x.accueil.html
Germany	http://www.deutsche-digitale-
Greece	http://www.nlg.gr/
Hungry	http://www.oszk.hu/index_hu.htm
Iceland	http://www.bok.hi.is/
India	http://www.nationallibrary.gov.in/
Indonesia	http://www.pnri.go.id/default.aspx
Iran	http://www.nlai.ir/
Ireland	http://www.nli.ie/

Country	Web site
Israel	http://www.jnul.huji.ac.il/heb/index.html
Italy	http://www.bncrm.librari.beniculturali.it/
Japan	http://www.ndl.go.jp/
Korea,	http://www.nl.go.kr/index.php
Luxembourg	http://www.bnl.public.lu/fr/index.html
Malaysia	http://www.pnm.my/index.php?id=50
Mexico	http://biblional.bibliog.unam.mx/bib/biblioteca. html
Netherlands	http://www.kb.nl/
New	http://www.natlib.govt.nz/
Norway	http://www.nb.no/
Peru	http://www.bnp.gob.pe/portalbnp/
Philippines	http://web.nlp.gov.ph/nlp/
Poland	http://www.bn.org.pl/
Portugal	http://www.bnportugal.pt/
Romania	http://www.bibnat.ro/
Russia	http://www.nlr.ru/
Saudi Arabia	http://www.kfnl.org.sa/
Singapore	http://www.nlb.gov.sg/
South Africa	http://www.nlsa.ac.za/NLSA/
Spain	http://www.bne.es/es/Inicio/index.html
Sweden	http://www.kb.se/
Switzerland	http://www.nb.admin.ch/

Country	Web site
Syria	http://www.alassad-library.gov.sy/
Thailand	http://www.nlt.go.th/th_index.htm
Turkey	http://www.mkutup.gov.tr/
Ukraine	http://www.nbuv.gov.ua/
United Kingdom	http://www.bl.uk/
United States	http://www.loc.gov/index.html
Vatican City	http://www.vaticanlibrary.va/
Venezuela	http://www.bnv.gob.ve/

Major Digitized Collections

In addition to libraries, a number of other cultural institutions such as museums and archives are creating digital libraries. For example, the Smithsonian has a wonderful Web site with a wide variety of resources available for viewing and downloading. The Smithsonian has set for itself four grand challenges:

- Unlocking the mysteries of the universe
- Understanding and sustaining a bio-diverse planet
- Valuing world cultures
- Understanding the American experience.

These are admirable goals indeed. Depending upon what your interests are, the Smithsonian is positioning a wide variety of Web-accessible resources. Thus, if you are:

- **A visitor** in one of the Smithsonian museums you might want to see additional resources using a mobile device while you are in front of a particular exhibit
- **A teacher** you might want your students to see (and experience) a variety of resources including photos, audio and video clips, and animations
- **An enthusiast** who wants to learn more about ..... (well, you name it!)
- **A scholar** who would like to gain access (remotely) to some portion of the Smithsonian's collections of artifacts and other resources.

The Smithsonian wants to provide access to its resources for individuals and others who would rather work together collaboratively.

Project Gutenberg

Project Gutenberg publishes eText versions of books (and other materials) not covered by copyright. The text of a book of interest to a volunteer is either manually entered or scanned and converted to text using optical character recognition (OCR) conversion software. However, the scanned image is not saved but rather only an ASCII (the American Standard Code for Information Interchange) file is saved. Currently about 33,000 books (mostly novels) are available in several languages. In addition to creating the text, other volunteers proofread the text to ensure accuracy and then load the file online.

Digital Resources from Museums

Organization	Description
Smithsonian http://www.si.edu/Exhibitions/Search/Virtual	The Smithsonian Institution—the world's largest museum and research complex—includes 19 museums and galleries and the National Zoological Park.
IMLS Digital Collections & Content http://imlsdcc.grainger.uiuc.edu/	Descriptions and links to digital resources developed by Institute of Museums & Library Services (IMLS) grantees.
U.S. Holocaust Memorial Museum http://www.ushmm.org/research/library/weblinks/?content=digital resources	Links to 13 Web sites dedicated to providing materials related to the holocaust.
Heard Museum http://www.heard.org/library/index.html	The Billie Jane Baguley Library and Archives of the Heard Museum is a comprehensive research facility that includes information about indigenous art and cultures from around the world and an unparalleled resource file containing information about more than 25,000 Native American artists.

Digital Resources from Museums - continued

Organization	Description
Digital History http://www.digitalhistory. uh.edu/images.cfm	Provides an extensive list of links to sites pertaining to United States history.
England's JISC Index of Digital Media Resources http://www.jiscdigitalmed ia.ac.uk/crossmedia/advic e/finding-subject-specific-digital-media-resources/	The purpose of this Web site is to provide a subject-specific guide to finding digital media resources with links to a number of useful websites.
British Museum http://www.britishmuseu m.org/the_museum/depar tments.aspx	A wide variety of digital resources are accessible via the British Museum.
National Galley of Canada http://www.gallery.ca/eng lish/319.htm	In addition to providing access to their own extensive collection of digital content, links are provided to other Canadian art resources.
Teacher Tap http://eduscapes.com/tap /topic35a.htm	Provides an extensive list of digital and virtual museums from around the world.

64

Summary

"The supposed universal library, then,

will not be a seamless mass of books,

easily linked and studied together,

but a patchwork of interfaces and databases,

some open to anyone with a computer and WiFi,

others closed to those without access or money.

The real challenge now is how to chart the tectonic plates

of information that are crashing into one another and

then learn to navigate the new landscapes

they are creating."

Anthony Grafton 2007

At first glance, the digitization of books and other materials seems like a no-brainer. More content is accessible to all for searching. Yet, like almost all technologies, there are positive and negative implications for the mass digitization of books and other items. Clearly, the law of unintended consequences is alive and well.

The ability to search the full text of millions of books has a transformative value to what it searches. Rather than simply searching the contents of bibliographic records, the user is now searching the full text plus the associated metadata of millions of books. A search not only uncovers the key words used in the search but also the value of connections. As people discover, comment upon, and discuss a particular book, author, concept, sentence, and paragraph, the links between the original and the new additional content will grow. The value of any digitized work thus increases the more it is shared.

With very few exceptions, almost all digital libraries are organized by their intellectual content or disciplinary focus. Funding for the creation of these digital libraries, be they science, medicine, or the humanities, often require a very narrow disciplinary focus. These disciplinary-focused digital libraries can present barriers to the non-specialist, as they will likely be unfamiliar with the discipline's subject content and vocabulary for expressing concepts within the discipline. Consider the needs and experience from the perspective of a doctor or nurse compared to the layperson when searching *Medline*. Serving these different needs presents real challenges to the designers of a digital library.

The other interesting observation is that the experience of using a digital library from the user's perspective is in many ways analogous to using a physical library today. That is, when visiting several different libraries the customer must learn to adapt to the library's catalog, classification system (Dewey, Library of Congress, others), and how the collection is physically organized in order to locate one or more desired items. So too, the user experience is radically different when using a digital library as the user interface for searching and browsing the digital resources varies. So even in the digital environment, the definition of a library catalog – a place where bibliographic records and resources get lost alphabetically – remains true.

The implications for every library of almost free and easy access to a major portion of the world's published books are enormous. The value of the local paper copy of a book in the library will become less and less important over time. As more eBooks are published the value of the pBook (print book) will decline. This reality raises important issues for all types of libraries.

Perhaps the foundational question that this raises is how does the local library provide value to its customers when so much content is now available online (and more digital content is being added all the time)?

Survival Guide Tips

Survival is dependent, in part, upon having the right clothing that is appropriate for the environment – desert, beach, mountains, deep snow, forest and so forth. Thus, being prepared for several eventualities improves your likely survival. This is particularly true as your organization moves from being a hybrid library to a digital library.

- Being aware of what digitization projects have been completed and are currently ongoing is important.

- Assessing your library's unique materials for possible digitization is an important first step in the process to create a digital library.

- Explore the possibility of collaborating with other similar libraries to digitize materials so that efforts are not duplicated.

Chapter 4

Acquiring Information

> *"Where is the life we have lost in living?*
>
> *Where is the wisdom we have lost in knowledge?*
>
> *Where is the knowledge we have lost in information?"*
>
> T.S. Eliot

Historically, libraries have purchased books and other materials to create a collection of quality and useful resources. As the owner of these materials a library would set policies for the borrowing and use of these materials while acknowledging that the copyright owner still retained some rights. For example, while an individual might make a photocopy of a page or two or .... it was expected that the library would pay a copyright fee for the privilege of making photocopies of a chapter or two or .... for students in a class.

The whole purpose of the library was to organize this physical collection and make the resources available to the customer. Over time, a series of processes were developed to acquire, catalog, and shelve the collection. The collection was organized in some intellectual manner using a classification system and the primary finding tool for the customer was the library's catalog. As the breadth of the publishing industry expanded (scientific journals and books; popular magazines, newspapers, and books; audio and video content – tapes, CDs, DVDs, MP3 files; special collections; and so forth) libraries coped by providing more indexing and finding tools (Books in Print and so forth). One of the unintended consequences of providing more tools was that the information seeking process became more complicated. In order to complete a comprehensive search, it was necessary to use a variety of tools. The result of this complexity is that more and more information became hidden (and not used).

As a library's collection grew larger and larger, the resources available to the user of the library became increasingly invisible to the user. Most users spend less than an hour when visiting a library and thus only focus on how to quickly find the resources they are interested in. From the perspective of the typical user, a library's collection is much like an iceberg – only 10 percent of the iceberg is visible on the surface while 90 percent hides below the water line.

Faculty members, graduate students and others used to rely exclusively on the library for the scholarly materials needed for research and teaching. However, as scholars have been able to access and download needed materials directly online, the library is being increasingly disintermediated from the research process. A series of surveys of faculty members from universities across the US have shown that scholars rely less on the library as a starting point for locating information (gateway) but that faculty value the library since it pays to provide access to electronic resources (the buyer function) and as a repository of resources or an archive (Schonfeld and Housewright 2010).

Libraries use a variety of tools to acquire and receive physical materials for the library. The integrated library system (ILS) provides two modules that assist the library in completing these tasks in a productive manner – Acquisitions and Serials Control.

See sidebar at the end of this chapter on the EOS Acquisitions and Serials modules.

With the introduction of online access to electronic content (initially electronic copies of journals or a group of journals selected since they were focused on a similar disciplinary subject), libraries could no longer purchase the intellectual content but rather they licensed access to the content.

Electronic Resource Management System

According to the Digital Library Federation, an electronic resource management system (ERMS) is "a system that supports management of the information and workflows necessary to efficiently select, evaluate, acquire, maintain, renew/cancel and provide informed access to e-resources in accordance with their business and license terms."

Electronic resources follow a set of business processes, as they become a part of the library's service offerings. These processes involve a life cycle that involves a specific workflow that is distributed across several staff members. These typical workflows include:

- **Consideration** – The library becomes aware of an electronic resource that is deemed worthy of further consideration. In order to proceed to the next step, the library needs to obtain some very specific information. Such information includes the title of the journal, whether the journal title is part of an aggregated database, other titles included as a part of the aggregated database, and so forth. A key feature is that the ERMS provides access to a comprehensive knowledgebase of all potential electronic resources not just those created by the library.

- **Trial** – The majority of electronic content publishers will provide access to a product on a temporary basis in order to provide the library with hands-on experience. The trial access typically involves registering the IP addresses associated with the institution, the provision of temporary username and a password to allow access for evaluation purposes. The duration of the trial is typically a few weeks.

- **Negotiation** – When the decision is made to license an electronic resource, the two parties work together towards an agreement on product options, pricing, and other details.

- **License** – A license agreement is signed that documents all of the agreements between the online provider and the library. This agreement specifies the terms of use, price, restrictions and other details.

- **Financial** – Once the license agreement is signed, the vendor will render an invoice for the product to the library. The ERMS system will track the payment progress and produce reports to help manage the library's budget.

- **Active Use & Monitoring** – Once the library starts to use an electronic resource, the library will receive statistics on a monthly basis about usage. These statistics can be provided on a paper report or downloaded from the publisher/vendor each month. The use of COUNTER (Counting Online Usage of NeTworked Electronic Resources) provides a uniform approach to making the statistical information from the various eJournal providers consistent in terms of how data is defined, gathered, and reported. A library should ensure that each of its electronic journal provider's is Release 3 COUNTER compliant. While library staff can log in each month to download COUNTER statistics for each vendor, a much more productive approach is to utilize a computer-to-computer communication protocol called SUSHI (Standardized Usage Statistics Harvesting Initiative - a NISO standard [Z39.93-2007]) to automatically retrieve the reports.

The data about the use of each product allows the library to determine its value as well as spotting technical problems that may arise. For example, if use statistics suddenly drop, it may reflect a technical problem that must be addressed.

- **Renewal/Deselection** – The time of renewal provides the library with the opportunity to assess the value of the electronic resource. If the actual use of a resource falls below expectations or the price increase being asked by the provider is too large, the library may want to cancel or deselect an existing electronic resource. An

ERMS will produce a report that provides a cost per use for each electronic resource used by the library.

- There are two broad approaches that a library may follow in selecting and implementing an ERMS:

- Licensing a software package, hosting the software on a server at the library and paying an annual software maintenance fee. The software can be provided by a commercial vendor, acquired for a nominal fee – or it may be free via an open source option. It should be noted that this latter option requires installation of equipment and a computer programmer to implement and maintain the system.

- Choosing a solution in which the library pays an annual subscription fee for the use of the software, where the ERMS system is hosted remotely. Sometimes this solution is called an Application Service Provider (ASP) service or Software as a Service (SaaS). This approach typically offers the advantages of lower total-cost-of-ownership and ready access to new features.

The **EOS.WEB® Electronic Resource Management** (ERM) module has been specifically designed to empower knowledge managers to effectively manage all electronic resources and Web Subscriptions, such as: electronic journals, databases, and electronic books. ERM makes it possible to completely streamline the entire electronic resource management process, from a review cycle for the resource record, to purchasing, publishing, and renewing a resource—all with one easy-to-use solution. Some of its features include:

- Filtered list control so library staff can easily manage resources

- View all ERM records or display records according to status: *pending, reviewed, purchased, published, renewed, or upcoming renewal*

- Force or passively allow the display of license agreements as patrons use a resource

- Retrieve records by name, title, statement, or vendor

- Edit, delete, or view the bibliographic record from the List Screen

- Edit the Web Subscription, edit the order, report problems with a subscription, email stakeholders, or renew a resource

- Enable or disable authorization to add, delete, and edit ERM records on a by-user basis

Searchable

The EOS.Web ERM module is so efficient that the electronic resource can be linked to the bibliographic record and Web Subscription, making it even easier for patrons to find the information they are looking for in your online catalog. To further increase an electronic resource's accessibility, you can also define a classification scheme for the bibliographic record.

ERM is tightly integrated with the Classification Management module, which allows you to determine which electronic

EOS.Web ERM - continued

resources display in search results and what items a patron can view from the collection. You control how your electronic resources are found by your patrons and how the information is presented through your Web OPAC. ERM simplifies the way your patrons gather electronic resources and perfects the way you manage your digital collections.

Organized

In addition to the increased searchability and usability of your electronic resources, ERM stores all record-specific information for a resource. Stored within the ERM record itself are all of the basic subscription information for the electronic resource, including: the license agreement, terms of use, and security concerns associated with the resource—so you don't have to manage this information separately. ERM intelligently organizes your digital library, and makes it easy to track and refine your e-resources.

Collaborative

ERM enables professional collaboration between you and your stakeholders. With ERM, managing the approval phase of e-resources is streamlined so you can be as efficient as possible. You determine the approval process, and ERM complies by allowing specific phases to be completed before a new phase can begin. ERM also enables library staff to solicit responses directly from other stakeholder groups. Stakeholders can manage and submit responses through the EOS.Web OPAC, and regardless if they approve, reject, or request more information, the library staff receives stakeholder responses by email, ensuring a quicker response-rate and shortened decision-making cycle.

ERM is a world-class, flexible, and continuously enhanced solution that is certain to help you effectively manage your digital collections.

Providing Access

Libraries provide access to this electronic content by listing the journal name or the name of the database on the library's Web site. The individual user who wants access to these electronic resources needs to be authenticated (has a library card or other valid identification) so that the terms of the licensing agreement with the vendor are followed.

Over the last ten years, the growth of the library's budget devoted to the licensing of electronic resources has steadily increased. For example, the following chart shows the total expenditures for electronic resources reported by ACRL academic libraries. Since 2004, total expenditures have risen from slightly more than $300 million to over $1 billion in 2009.

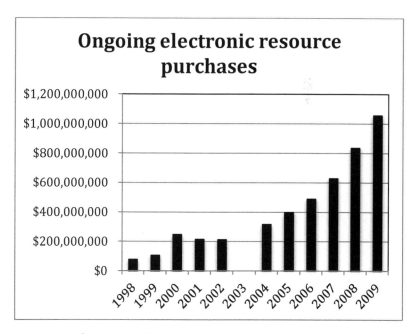

Note: 2003 data not available

A series of surveys indicated that most users of electronic resources, even after logging in to gain access to electronic resources using the library's Web site, are unaware of the costs and effort required to make these resources accessible. Thus, more and more of the library's services are becoming even more invisible. For example, the OCLC Perceptions report (2005) surveyed 3,348 respondents from seven English-speaking countries. This report found that 84 percent of individuals started a search for information using an Internet search engine (most used Google). Only 1 percent used their academic or public library as a starting point! And respondents rated search engines higher than libraries in terms of quality and quantity of information.

Surprisingly only 16 percent of respondents had ever used an online database and only 30 percent had ever used a library Web site. These results are contrasted with the fact that 72 percent had used free search engines such as Google. A Pew Internet & American Life Project report (2002) noted, 55 percent of users completely agree that Google supplies worthwhile information while only 31 percent for library databases. Furthermore, library-supplied information is not trusted any more than free Internet-based information.

It must always be remembered that *convenience trumps everything* during the information search process!

One of the continuing challenges facing all libraries is that the library "brand" can be captured in one word – books! Yet most libraries devote little or none of their budget to marketing in an effort to suggest that the library is more than books. Most information consumers are not aware of, and do not use, the library's electronic information resources. And college students, who are intensive users of the library, indicate that their library's collections (physical and electronic) do not meet their information needs. Most students use an information-seeking and research strategy driven by efficiency and predictability for managing and controlling all of the information resources available to them on college campuses (Head and Eisenberg 2010).

Web Scale Discovery

Recently some libraries have signed up for a new service with the generic name of Web Scale Discovery. A Web Scale Discovery service is a very large, centralized, pre-aggregated index of electronic journals plus the local library's online catalog that can be quickly searched by the end user. A Web Scale Discovery service provides discovery and delivery services that have the following traits:

- Content. The content from electronic journals (at the article level) are gathered together (harvested) with the permission of the publisher or aggregator and a large centralized index is created.
- Discovery. A single Google-like search box is provided (as well as advanced search capabilities) and the search results are ranked by relevancy. Thus, the user need not log on and search multiple eJournal databases – each with their own unique user search interface.
- Delivery. The results are provided in rank order of relevancy along with other cues to facilitate the user's navigation – faceted navigation might be provided.

- Flexibility. The customer library of these services has much more latitude to customize the services in order to better meet the needs of the library's customers.

Currently there are five Web Scale Discovery services: OCLC WorldCat Local, Serials Solutions Summon, EBSCO Discovery Services, Innovative Interfaces Encore Synergy, and Ex Libris Primo Central (Vaughn 2011).

Sources of Information

Currently libraries obtain digital content by:

- Licensing access to digital content provided by a third party or vendor
- Digitizing content of existing special collections or the library's general collection, e.g., books, photographs, personal papers, and so forth
- Harvesting the digital content or its metadata from distributed digital resources (other digital libraries). In some cases, after the metadata is harvested, the system provides a link to the remote digital content.

It is important to remember that the quality of the digital object can serve several possible purposes. These include:

- **Protection of the Originals.** Digital copies of sufficient quality can be used in lieu of handling and browsing through original sources. Examples of original sources include older photographs, clippings, vertical files, manuscripts, personal correspondence and so forth. Preservation objectives are achieved since the handling of the originals is minimized.

- **Represent Originals**. The digital objects are captured in such detail that the system can be used to fulfill most if not all of the research and learning needs. The ability to "see" the digital object as if you were handling the original frees researchers from having to travel to conduct their research.

- **Transcend Originals**. It is also possible to capture a very high quality digital image that then allows the digital object to be used in ways that would be impossible with the original source. The imaging process and subsequent "editing" of the digital image allows the negative effects of aging, use and environmental damage to be overcome and to restore details that would otherwise have escaped notice.

One of the challenges for libraries is the degree to which the search process (or browsing) is simplified and integrated. That is, is it necessary for the user to select the type of digital content they are interested in (electronic journals, digital books, audio and/or video, animations and so forth) or will the system conduct a simultaneous search of all resources on behalf of the user?

Interoperability

The objective of interoperability is to build a coherent set of services for users from components and digital objects that are technically different and managed by different organizations.

Three levels of interoperability have been identified by Arms et al (2003) and they include:

1. Federated
2. Harvesting
3. Gathering.

Federated, sometimes referred to as federated searching or cross searching, sends search criteria to multiple (remote) digital libraries and the results are gathered, combined, and presented to the user (Alipour-Hafezi et al 2010). In library land, Z39.50 has long been a standard for federated searching of library online catalogs. The Z39.50 protocol is a client-server based model, where the server responds to queries from the client. Another federated search protocol has been developed at Stanford University and is called SDLIP – Simple Digital Library Interoperability Protocol.[1] Additional federated protocols have been developed by other organizations.

The *harvesting model* allows participants to take small efforts to enable some basic shared services without a formal set of agreements. For example, the Open Archives Initiative (OAI) is based on the idea of metadata harvesting or sharing. The OAI model allows a library to make its metadata about its collections available in a simple exchange format. The resulting shared metadata can then be added to the local digital library service in order to improve information discovery. The OAI model minimizes cost by using a simple HTTP-based protocol. A standard OAI-based

---

[1] More information about SDLIP available at
http://dbpubs.stanford.edu:8091/~testbed/doc2/SDLIP/

protocol has been developed and is called the Open Archives Initiative Protocol for Metadata Harvesting (OAI-PMH).

Using the harvesting model, a library asks one or more libraries to interoperate with one another. The result for the user is that a search for content using one digital library retrieves information regardless of where the digital content is stored. A number of libraries and other organizations, including NASA, are using OAI on a daily basis.

The *gathering model* is a base model of interoperability that gathers openly accessible information using a Web search engine. The good news is that the resources of the digital library are accessible via a search engine such as Google. The bad news is that the digital library resources are not being shared with other digital libraries using the OAI-PMH. CiteSeer (http://citeseer.ist.psu.edu/) is a good example of a digital library built automatically by gathering publicly accessible information.

Regardless of the interoperability model chosen, among the issues that will need to be confronted are semantic differences and the use of different vocabularies used to describe a collection or individual digital object. The issues are particularly challenging when attempting to share information among and between digital libraries, archives, historical societies, and museums (Lopatin 2006).

Summary

The challenges facing libraries when they acquire content for their digital library can be daunting. As each library provides more and digital content, the value of its existing physical collections diminish as evidenced by declining use. Thus, the visibility of the library fades into the distance. The challenge is how does the library create and maintain value in today's digital milieu – and tomorrow's even more digital environment? More about this topic may be found later in this book.

Survival Guide Tips

Sometimes having the correct tool will mean the difference between life and death – especially in a survival situation. One critical tool is an all-purpose knife. The knife will come in handy when branches need to be cut, fish need to be cleaned, and so forth. So too in a digital library!

- Increasingly the library is being called upon to manage the complicated process of licensing electronic content – eJournals and databases.

- Each library must insist that the vendors providing usage reports of their electronic resources do so in a format that is Release 3 COUNTER compliant.

- While libraries consider the quality of their collections (both physical and electronic) the principle reason for the use of the library, in reality the user is primarily concerned with convenience.

- A digital library object will not only protect the original from future damage it will also, in some cases, transcend the original by providing more detail and ways to examine the original using information technology.

- The Open Archives Initiative Protocol for Metadata Harvesting (OAI-PMH) provides a way to harvest metadata from another digital library so that the user becomes aware of an extended set of resources that may be of value.

EOS.Web® Acquisitions

Manage Detailed Acquisitions Tasks

The customizable EOS.Web Acquisitions module tracks and processes the purchasing of library materials through ordering, claiming, receiving, and invoicing.

Simplifies Acquisitioning Workflow Tasks

EOS.Web Acquisitions has an intuitive, easy-to-use interface that makes ordering and tracking purchases of items manageable, even for multi-institutional and multi-fund, shared acquisitions. An interactive, integrated record structure provides for transactions in one record to automatically be updated in all EOS.Web modules, thus simplifying acquisitioning workflows. For example, when an item is recorded as received, vendor statistics, holdings, and financial files are automatically updated, including when item record changes are made. Tasks for acquisitions such as online periodicals, online journals, law reports, maps, video, and audio are automated for you, such as: pre-order searching, ordering, claiming, cancellation, payment, invoicing, fund accounting, vendor accounting, currency control, statistics and report compilation.

Fund Account File

The Fund Account file is updated automatically to indicate file encumbrances and debits as a result of actions on the acquisition file. At a glance, you'll see amount budgeted, amount encumbered, amount expended, uncommitted balance, balance from previous year, encumbrances carried from previous year, cash balance, and supplementary budget appropriations.

EOS.Web® Serials

Automated Serial Prediction

The EOS.Web Serials module enables you to control receipt of journals, series and supplements, no matter what their publishing schedule is or location. Built-in issue receipt prediction functionality accommodates a wide variety of regular and irregular publishing schedules, which makes management of both predictable and unpredictable, unstructured journals quick and easy.

Serials management is made quick and easy, giving libraries and information centers the ability to not only catalog a serials title, but also to predict, receive, and claim individual serial issues in addition to the ability to claim missing issues and create custom routing slips. This is due to support for the MARC serials holdings standard used to track issues.

Automated Serials Check-in

Serial check-in is made quick and accurate. If the issue to be received is not the predicted issue, the system predicts and displays the chronology and enumeration of future issues. Automated serials easily handles special or duplicate issues, supports check-in of irregular patterns, supports multiple copies, tracks issue location, prints TOC labels and routing slips, tracks damaged issues, and provides editable holding summary statements.

Built-in MARC Editor

EOS.Web Enterprise has the MARC editor at the Serial Copy level to edit MARC Holdings records in raw MARC.

EOS.Web Serials - continued

Customizable Routing Lists

Journal, TOC route slips, and TOC labels are supported in addition to the ability to create multiple routing slips for each copy of a serial. Customizable routing list information includes the serial title, name, and location of the recipient. An unlimited number of modifiable patrons can be included on a list.

Customizable Web OPAC Integration

Full integration of the EOS.Web OPAC catalogs makes check-in information immediately available to the online catalog, making it easy to see if there are missing issues. Location information and public notes display with the holdings statement. Additionally, you can build links from the serials bibliographic record to electronic magazines, electronic journals, online periodicals, and more, making it easy for your patrons to immediately see if an article in a specific journal is in the library.

Simplified Serials Bindings

Serials bindery functionality includes the ability to automatically move the serial set into the bindery cycle, provides bindery instructions, and enables shipment tracking of the set until the bound set is received by the library.

Customizable, Automated Claiming

Claiming issues is automated by providing the ability to establish parameters for determining dates when claims should be made, including the ability to define the interval between the predicted arrival date and the claim date. At any time authorized staff can override claims parameters (in order to prevent a claim, or delay the date, or to generate a claim independently of the parameters).

Chapter 5

Organizing Information

"That which today calls itself science
gives us more and more information,
an indigestible glut of information,
and less and less understanding."

Edward Abbey

Perhaps the primary value libraries have historically provided to their customers is that they organized the information resources they had acquired. This process of organization is called cataloging. A bibliographic record is created that describes the physical or electronic item in the library. A series of cataloging standards are typically used to create this bibliographic record. The records are then placed in a catalog that is used by library staff and customers in order to locate desired items. Historically, three main indexes were provided – author, title, and subject – but with automation came the use of additional indexes, especially the keyword index.

For many users, the library catalog is a place where bibliographic records get lost alphabetically!

Cataloging

A bibliographic record that is created to describe an item in a library collection uses a series of standards to properly construct the record. The bibliographic record is a surrogate for the actual item itself. Until recently, the primary standard was the Anglo-American Cataloging Rules or AACR2. AACR2 bibliographic records created using a computer were often referred to as MARC records – Machine Readable Cataloging records.

As libraries moved into the digital environment as the result of the Internet (the Internet has indeed changed every-thing), several shortcomings were evident with regard to AACR2. These issues included:

- Cataloging descriptions are based foremost upon a resource's format (its tangible or intangible carrier) rather than on its intellectual or artistic content
- The ambiguity of what constitutes a "work," especially when multiple authors are present
- The difficulties of controlling digital content in a variety of forms and greater variety for storing, manipulating and displaying bibliographic records
- Little flexibility in describing a work given the rigidity of the majority of the cataloging rules.

Efforts to revise AACR2 led to the decision to base the new cataloging standard using the International Federation of Library Associations (IFLA) documents *Functional Requirements for Bibliographic Records* (FRBR) and *Functional Requirements for Authority Data* (FRAD). These two documents articulate an explicit model that includes an entity-relationship (ER) model. This model promotes a broader view of metadata as a network of data that can interact with any other community's data. Thus, metadata developments that are compatible with Web-based technologies promote the interconnections of libraries with other organizations.

The resulting revision was called *Resource Description and Access* (RDA). RDA is designed to cover description and access for all digital and analog resources and reflects the constructs of object-oriented or relational databases. The author(s) of a work is linked to the title, which in turn is linked to a publication statement and subject headings. These relationships are shown in Figure 5-1.

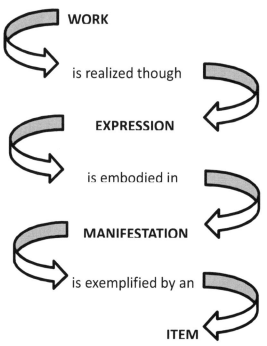

WORK

is realized though

EXPRESSION

is embodied in

MANIFESTATION

is exemplified by an

ITEM

Figure 5-1 FRBR Entities

The four entities and their relationships are included in the FRBR model as shown in Figure 5-1. These include:

- **Work** is the intellectual or artistic creation as an abstract entity
- **Expression** is the realization of a work in a particular form – a particular language or notation
- **Manifestation** is the physical embodiment of an expression of work (this level is the one represented in bibliographic records)
- **Item** is a single exemplar of a manifestation (a copy if you will).

FRBR maps these relationships to specific user tasks:

- To **find** entities that correspond to the user's stated query
- To **identify** an entity
- To **select** an entity that is appropriate to the user's needs
- To **acquire** or **obtain** access to the entity described.

Using the FRBR conceptual model as the foundation, the RDA code becomes a content standard and not a display standard. Resource Description & Access is divided into ten sections – the first four sections are focused on establishing the FRBR/FRAD entities for the library catalog (bibliographic and authority record data); while the remaining sections describe the relationships between entities. The ten RDA sections include:

1. Recording Attributes of Manifestation and Item
2. Recording Attributes of Work and Expression

3. Recording Attributes of Person, Family, and Corporate Body
4. Recording Attributes of Concept, Object, Event, and Place
5. Recording Primary Relationships between Work, Expression, Manifestation, and Item
6. Recording Relationships to Persons, Families, and Corporate Bodies Associated with a Resource
7. Recording Subject Relationships
8. Recording Relationships between Works, Expressions, Manifestations, and Items
9. Recording Relationships between Persons, Families, and Corporate Bodies
10. Recording Relationships between Concepts, Objects, Events, and Places.

Not surprisingly, FRBR and RDA introduce a whole new vocabulary for catalogers (and almost all other librarians). And remember that AACR2 is based on the concept of a unit record system (the item) while for FRBR and RDA the focus is on the work. Table 5-1 provides some indication of the shift in vocabulary under the new RDA system.

AACR2 Terms	RDA Terms
Heading	Access point
Added entry	Access point
Authorized heading	Preferred access point
See (cross) references	Variant access point
Main entry	No RDA equivalent
Uniform title	Preferred title
Authority control	A separate model

Table 5-1. Shift in Cataloging Vocabulary

The intent of RDA is to make users of library catalogs more aware of the relationships between works and their creators by clearly showing the different editions, translations, or physical formats of a work.

In a similar manner, FRAD – Functional Requirements for Authority Data extends the FRBR model as shown in Figure 5-2. The FRAD entities are important because they support collocation and navigation and these relationships are crucial for the new generations of online catalogs.

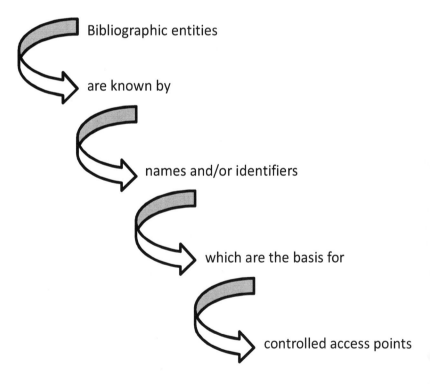

Bibliographic entities

are known by

names and/or identifiers

which are the basis for

controlled access points

Figure 5-2 FRAD

Dublin Core

Recognizing that many digitization projects were going to be completed using non-librarians as well as acknowledging the complexity of the existing bibliographic records, a group gathered in Dublin, Ohio to create a simplified record that has come to be called metadata – or data describing other data. The resulting Dublin Core metadata record has fifteen fields and its primary purpose is resource discovery since all elements are optional and repeatable.

A Simplified View of Dublin Core

The Dublin Core Metadata Element Set is a vocabulary of fifteen properties for use in resource description. The name "Dublin" is due to its origin at a 1995 invitational workshop in Dublin, Ohio. "Core" because its elements are broad and generic, usable for describing a wide range of resources.

Label	Definition
Contributor	An entity responsible for making contributions to the resource.
Coverage	The spatial or temporal topic of the resource, the spatial applicability of the resource, or the jurisdiction under which the resource is relevant.
Creator	An entity primarily responsible for making the resource.
Date	A point or period of time associated with an event in the lifecycle of the resource.
Description	An account or explanation of the resource.
Format	The file format, physical medium, or dimensions of the resource.
Identifier	An unambiguous reference to the resource within a given context.
Language	A language of the resource.
Publisher	An entity responsible for making the resource available.
Relation	A related resource.
Rights	Information about rights held in and over the resource.
Source	A related resource from which the described resource is derived.
Subject	The topic of the resource.
Title	A name given to the resource.
Type	The nature or genre of the resource.

For a more detailed explanation of Dublin Core visit
http://dublincore.org/documents/dces/

Dublin Core is also extensible in that additional elements and encoding schemes can be added. Some of these additional qualified elements include Audience, Instructional Method, Rights Holder, and Provenance. The additional Dublin Core element refinements are shown below.

Dublin Core Element Refinements

Abstracts	Is referenced by
Access rights	Is replaced by
Alternative	Is required by
Audience	Issued
Available	IS version of
Bibliographic citation	License
Conforms to	Mediator
Created	Medium
Date accepted	Modified
Date copyrighted	Provenance
Date submitted	References
Education level	Replaces
Extent	Requires
Has format	Rights holder
Has part	Spatial
Has version	Table of contents
Is format of	Temporal
Is part of	Valid

The Dublin Core Metadata Initiative is based on the Resource Descriptive Framework (RDF). RDF is a simple model that only defines three types of data: literal values (free text), structured values (text with structure), and identifies in the Uniform Resource Identifier (URI). RDF is used as a general method for the modeling of information that is implemented in Web resources and was developed by the World Wide Web Consortium.

RDF is being used to develop a number of metadata standards and applications. Two are of particular note:

- Simple Knowledge Organization System (SKOS) is a way to present organized data such as thesauri, classification systems, and subject heading schemes. SKOS is being used by the Library of Congress to implement their subject headings on the Web.
- The Web Ontology Language (OWL) provides additional functionality for the relationships between terms in a vocabulary.

Many types of metadata exist and each type serves different purposes. For example, a digital object might have:

- *Descriptive metadata* including a "bibliographic" description (including subject access), possible content ratings or evaluation information
- *Administrative metadata* relates to the terms and conditions of use, provenance (source, date of creation and so forth), file type, transactions (date of deposit, date of request, object interrelationships and so forth)

- *Structural metadata* concerns information that makes the object useable – for example, page turning in an electronic book
- *Preservation metadata* for information related to long-term preservation of objects.

It is also important to recognize that since Dublin Core was designed for the digital environment, all of the tools are based on the XML standard – eXtensible Markup Language – the language of the Web.

EOS.Web® Cataloging

EOS.Web Cataloging provides simplified yet powerful functionality to manage a library's bibliographic, authority, and item records. Its unmatched flexibility enables libraries to create a database of information that is tailored to their organization, thus improving access to information.

Useful links enable librarians to gain access to cataloger's reference tools, (e.g., Library of Congress' Cataloger's Desktop), and to download records from a bibliographic utility or CD-ROM database product in MARC format, thus improving cataloging efficiency.

EOS.Web supports the Bibliographic, Authority, and MARC Holdings standards in both the MARC21 and OCLC MARC formats. This functionality means that you can import authority records such as new Medical Subject Headings (MeSH) from authorities like the National Library of Medicine and have the EOS.Web system automatically update the linked bibliographic records.

EOS.Web Cataloging - continued

The flexible cataloging module also provides the ability for you to customize the MARC rules themselves, in addition to the ability to add text descriptions to MARC records and have that text be fully searchable. The 13 digit ISBN format is built into the module.

Customizable Catalog Database Content

The EOS.Web Catalog database is completely customizable to your collection. The bibliographic index building process accepts custom taxonomies, any MARC field, or any identifiable portion thereof that can be identified for inclusion in the index. Customizable data entry templates are also provided. Additionally you can:

- Easily customize the status of items in the catalog, including whether or not the item is OPAC viewable status or password only accessible
- Identify custom cross-references and authority files
- Enter unlimited notes for entry of custom taxonomy information such as table of contents, book jacket or back cover, or blurbs from a video jacket
- Create a group of custom research materials and make them available for searching, such as in-house created titles, new fiction titles list, new children's title list, or special cataloging record sets

Customizable and Personalized Security Settings

The EOS.Web system provides for extensive security restrictions including restrictions on operators who are allowed to add, delete, or modify the bibliographic record.

EOS.Web Cataloging - continued

Customizable Authority Control

You can additionally place restrictions on whether the database, collection, or item should be viewable by the public. Only authorized operators are allowed to add or change authority file entries.

Full MARC Authority records as defined by Library of Congress standards are easily handled, however EOS.Web also provides customizable authority files for desired fields (e.g., personal and corporate names, series, and subject headings) as well as for all defined cross-references for each.

Authority files permit appropriate "see" and "see also" cross-references to be displayed, indexed and maintained. Additionally, the Library can establish and maintain broader, narrower, related, earlier, later, etc. headings and references enabling protection against circular and blind "see" and "see also" cross references.

Dublin Core

Two Dublin Core templates are available in EOS.Web Enterprise. The Dublin Core MARC template allows for MARC import/export and original cataloging of MARC-based DC records. The Dublin Core KnowledgeBuilder template allows for import/ export from a CSV file and original cataloging in KnowledgeBuilder. Both options allow DC to fully integrate with your MARC collection. DC templates are based on Dublin Core Element Set Version 1.1 and can be modified by your library.

MODS

The Metadata Object Descriptive Standard (MODS) is simpler in design than a MARC bibliographic record but more robust than Dublin Core. MODS shares definitions with MARC and it does not assume any specific rules for description. The use of XML schema allows for flexibility and availability of freely available tools. Related items may be briefly or fully described by the same tags as are used for the item being cataloged. The emphasis of MODS is on access points over description.

While MODS elements generally inherit the semantics of MARC they do not assume the use of any specific rules for description. XML schema allows for flexibility and the use of freely available software tools. The MODS elements are:

• Title info	• Subject
• Name	• Classification
• Type of resource	• Related item
• Genre	• Identifier
• Origin info	• Location
• Language	• Access conditions
• Physical description	• Extension
• Abstract	• Record info
• Table of contents	• Root elements
• Target audience	• Note

MADS

MADS or the Metadata Authority Description Schema is a companion to MODS. MADS is an XML-based schema that may be used to provide metadata about agents (people, organizations), events and terms (topics, geographic, genres, and so forth). MADS is related to the MARC Authority Record format.

METS

METS or the Metadata Encoding and Transmission Standard is used as a wrapper for descriptive and technical, rights, preservation and other metadata. It enables resource retrieval, object validation, preservation actions, and rights management. METS is used to submit a digital object to a repository or for the interchange of digital objects between systems.

Other evolving standards of interest to librarians and the digital library environment include MIX (Metadata for Images in XML), PREMIS (Preservation Metadata Implementation Strategies), SRU (Search and Retrieval via URL) and textMD (technical metadata for text-based digital objects) that includes information about encoding information (quality, platform, software, agent), character information (character set, byte order and size), language and fonts, markup information, processing and textual notes, technical requirements for printing and viewing and page ordering and sequencing.

ONIX

ONIX, or the Online Information eXchange, is a set of related international standards for communication between computer systems. ONIX standards cover intellectual property rights in media content, usage permissions and prohibitions, and the registration of standard identifiers for works and their manifestations. ONIX for Books was the first and is the most widely used of these standards. ONIX allows for two levels of description: Level 1 has 82 elements while Level 2 has 235 elements of information in 24 categories.

MARC and ONIX are structurally and semantically different since they support different needs and were developed using different technologies. OCLC has developed a mapping of ONIX to MARC (Godby 2010).

EAD

Encoded Archival Description (EAD) uses a Document Type Definition (DTD) as a standard for encoding (creating metadata) archival finding aids using the Extensible Markup Language (XML). It is important to remember that EAD is a data structure and not a data content standard. EAD is a data communication format based on SGML/XML syntax.

DACS

Describing Archives: A Content Standard (DACS) is a set of rules for describing archives, personal papers, and manuscript collections that can be applied to all material types. The Society of American Archivists developed DACS.

VRA Core

VRA Core is a data standard for the description of works of visual culture as well as the images that document them. VRA Core as a metadata standard will work well as an extension schema for any METS object that contains images of cultural heritage resources.

Cataloging Schmataloging

Historically, library cataloging has relied on the "first order of information" concept described by David Weinberger in *Everything is Miscellaneous* (2007), the traditional understanding of the "collection" relies on the idea (and even necessity) that things belong in one particular place and one place only. However, the realities of digital access make this a 'requirement' that can be safely ignored as it is possible to "store" a digital object (conceptually at least) in multiple locations.

A library can describe the contents of its digital collections using Dublin Core or MODS or whatever standard is appropriate for the materials being digitized. This descriptive metadata is what people are using as they discover resources of possible interest.

After all, most users discover digital objects using the Internet rather than using the prescribed paths provided in a digital library's catalog. This means that Weinberger's "third order of information" can be utilized – that is, materials are not grouped at all but retain multiple, not pre-determined qualities (such as placement in a single collection). These qualities can then be searched and aggregated in various ways that make the most sense to the customer. Customer-focused groupings mean that the user will find more things of interest – serendipitous discovery.

Further, as with Flickr and other social media Web sites, users can add tags to a digital object that others may find to be more meaningful. Thus, the goal of any digital library should be to provide tools that encourage users to interact with the digital content and provide access to many more images, in many more ways. This allows the user to build context and connect with a larger community of users with similar interests.

Impact of Social Networks

The popularity of social networking sites is due, in large part, to the ability of the individual to add and modify existing content. Consider the popularity of Flickr that encourages people to download and display their photographs. The entire experience is enhanced in that people can add words to describe a picture posted by someone else. This process of adding words is called "tagging" and the tagging words or phrases are called "tags." For example, LibraryThing.com encourages people to "catalog" their own personal libraries as well as tag the contributions of others. The process of tagging has been given the name of "folksonomies" to reflect the collaborative process to annotate and classify collections. Folksonomies have also been called social indexing, social classification, social tagging, folk classification, distributed classification, free tagging, open tagging, and collaborative tagging. Folksonomies are created after the content has been "published" on the Internet while a taxonomy is a classification system that is created prior to materials being added to a collection. While some librarians may disagree, tagging and controlled vocabularies have a role in information discovery and are not mutually exclusive (Schwartz 2008).

The characteristics of user tagging that distinguish it from the traditional methods of description, annotation or categorization include:

- User-oriented
- Empowering

- Democratic
- Collaborative
- Distributed
- Dynamic
- Instructive
- Cheap (Furner 2008).

In a similar manner, sites such as Amazon.com encourage people to rate the items that they purchase and write reviews for books and videos. In short, tools are provided that facilitate the building of communities.

Libraries need to provide similar tools on their Web sites and in their library catalogs so that the library "experience" is enhanced through a collaborative and interactive relationship among people with similar interests. These tools should feed new content, annotations, and comments back to the digital library site that will benefit other users of the digital library (Bearman 2007).

Summary

The importance of metadata that is linked to a digital object cannot be over-emphasized. After all, the digital object is simply a collection of bits (called a bitmap) that cannot be found or understood without some level of metadata.

The description of a digital object is an important activity that historically librarians fulfilled on behalf of all library customers. However, as the Internet has moved increasingly into the social milieu, people expect to be able to add their "two cents" worth by tagging digital objects, rating digital objects as well as physical artifacts (for example, books reviews) and other community-building activities.

The sad reality is that digitization is still not considered a core function of most libraries. To have a larger impact in the life of users, the digital library must become more central to how the library delivers content and services. This presents a real challenge for any library. How can you ensure the automation tools are in place to make sure that the digital library plays a significant role in the life of people in their communities (geographic, academic or organizational)?

The answer to this challenge lies in four parts:

1. The library needs to spend less time creating "full" bibliographic descriptive records for books (moving from the detailed MARC record to the less structured Dublin Core or MODS record). Since the full text of books are now being indexed and searched, the need for a full bibliographic record is diminishing.
2. Index the complete content of a "born digital" document or the digitized content of existing analog library materials – books, journals, photos, audio, video and other materials
3. Provide links to related content from other digital libraries and museums
4. Work to provide a sense of context within the library's online catalog or Web site. This may require the library to provide a sense of time (a timeline) or place (links to maps) for the digital content contained within their catalog.

Survival Guide Tips

Adaptability is an important lesson in surviving in a rapidly changing environment. In the library world, the environment around libraries is clearly changing and some would suggest that change is in fact increasing. Thus, the following digital library survival tips.

- Many organizations have recognized the need to develop new standards for describing content in a digitally rich environment.

- The library profession has seen the adoption of Dublin Core and MODS as a replacement for the MARC record to describe objects in our increasingly digital world.

- Resource Description & Access has replaced AACR2 as the standard for creating a bibliographic record.

- Other library-related professions have created similar new standards – ONIX, EAD, and VRA Core to name a few.

- Library catalogs must allow users to contribute their own comments, reviews and tags that will only enrich the discovery process.

Suggested RDA Resources

- Chris Oliver. *Introducing RDA: A Guide to the Basics.* Chicago: ALA Editions, 2010.

- Amy Hart. *The RDA Primer: A Guide for the Occasional Cataloger.* Santa Barbara: Linworth, 2010.

- Shawne Miksa. *Introduction to Resource Description and Access.*

Learning More About Furr-Burr (FRBR)

- Arlene Taylor. *Understanding FRBR.* Westport, CN: Libraries Unlimited, 2007.

- Robert Maxwell. *FRBR: A Guide for the Perplexed.* Chicago: ALA Editions, 2008.

- Yin Zhang and Athene Salaba. *Implementing FRBR in Libraries.* New York: Neal-Schuman, 2009.

MARC, MARCXML, and MODS

MARC

[245] 10$aStones into schools:$bpromoting peace with education in Afghanistan and Pakistan /$cGreg Mortensen and Khaled Hosseini

MARCXML

```
<datafield tag="245" ind1="1" ind2="0">
 <subfield code="a">Stones into schools</subfield>
 <subfield code="b">promoting peace with education in Afghanistan and Pakistan</subfield>
 <subfield code="c">Greg Mortensen and Khaled Hosseini</subfield>
</datafield>
```

MODS

```
<titleinfo><title>Stones into schools</title>
 <subtitle>promoting peace with education in Afghanistan and Pakistan</subtitle>
<note type="statement of responsibility"> Greg Mortensen and Khaled Hosseini
```

Chapter 6

Finding Information

"Technology is so much fun
but we can drown in our technology.
The fog of information can drive out knowledge".

Daniel J. Boorstein

The enhanced access to remote research materials is one of the most – if not the most – important attribute of electronic resources. Improved access to digital materials provides a valuable contribution to a user community and will satisfy local, national and international scholars and individuals with an interest in a particular topic. Basically anything that can be done to make rare, historical, damaged or unique content accessible remotely makes the task of research that much easier.

From the perspective of a user of an online system, the process of searching can be frustrating indeed. For many users, the traditional library online catalog doesn't tend to order search results in a useful manner (for example, ranked by relevance) and the user interface is often clunky and sometimes downright confusing. Recently, Jean Bauer, a graduate student at the University of Virginia conducted a search for "Thomas Jefferson" using the library's online catalog (named Virgo) and was so frustrated with the results that she titled a bibliography "Meager Fruits of an Ongoing Fight with Virgo" (Parry 2009). The end result for many library users is that they give up and go somewhere else to get their information.

In almost all cases, the library catalog will only show the books, DVDs, CDs and some other materials contained within the library. The catalog will not show all of the articles to be found in the various paper and electronic journals that are subscribed to by the library – it will likely be necessary to search a fair number of other databases to find other pertinent information. Other searches will be necessary if you want to find information in one or more newspapers, the library's special collections, or on the Internet. In short, the information seeking process is frustrating, time-consuming and without any guarantee that the results will be accurate or comprehensive.

Google and Its Impact

"Numerous studies have shown users are often willing to sacrifice information quality for accessibility.

This fast food approach to information consumption drives librarians crazy. "Our information is healthier and tastes better too" they shout. But nobody listens.

We're too busy Googling."

Peter Morville

The popularity of Google and its search engine is attested to by the impact it has had in our language. "To Google" has become synonymous with did you find the answer to your question on the Internet by searching on Google? Google processes roughly 2 billion searches per day! Perhaps the biggest two impacts of Google is that people now expect a simple search box and that the results will be presented in the most useful way (ranked by relevance). In short, convenience always trumps quality!

The popularity of Google has significant implications for any library's online catalog. One important study compared the searches conducted at a university online catalog to the results from Google Books. All of the searches for one day were performed using Google Books – 1,596 searches in all. In the library's online catalog 295 searches retrieved no records (zero hits). Using Google Books, the same searches retrieved an average of 351 items! In every case, the number of items retrieved using Google Books vastly exceeded that of the library's online catalog emphasizing that information retrieval is more successful when you have more to search (all of the words in each book) versus the "brief" bibliographic record (Ludwig and Wells 2008). Thus, it is not surprising that "discovery" of information resources takes place outside of the library (and the library's online catalog).

However, more than Google is involved here. The whole online experience is being influenced by the positive user experience of the widely used transaction sites such as Amazon, eBay, Yahoo and others. Some have called this effect of rising user expectations as "Amazoogle" and "Googlezon" (Dempsey 2005). This case of rising user expectations while they are online has serious implications for libraries and library online systems.

However, it is important to recognize that an enormous amount of scholarly literature and other printed material is simply not findable through any electronic means, as it does not exist in digital form.

Given that discovery takes place outside of the library and the library's online catalog, optimizing a library's Web site becomes very important. Search engine optimization makes any Web site attractive to a search engine and improves its position in the rankings that are displayed to the user. Optimization is achieved by adding commonly used search terms to a Web site, removing barriers to the indexing bots used by search engines, and increasing link and social media popularity (JISC 2009).

Information Retrieval

Finding information is no easy task for many reasons. Words entered by the user are assumed to accurately represent the individuals real information need (this is not always the case) and the words themselves often have many different meanings – words are imprecise, indeterminate, vague, ambiguous and .... well, you get the picture. Words have synonyms, homonyms, and are often acronyms or contractions of two or more words.

George Zipf, a Harvard University linguistics professor, found that a few words occur quite frequently while many other words occur infrequently. Zipf suggested that there are two forces working in competition with one another – unification (general words with many meanings) and diversification (specific words with specific meaning (the jargon of a profession or academic discipline).

Thus, the fundamental challenge of any information retrieval or search system is to provide the most relevant documents, books, Web sites to the user without finding irrelevant materials. If an automated system has some idea of the aboutness of a search request (based on prior usage by a specific individual or the actions of a large number of other people then it can improve the entire experience for the user.

In the case of Google, it uses the metadata supplied by humans – that is it recognizes the links constructed by people from one Web site to others as an excellent indicator of aboutness.

But consider the problems experienced by people when searching. Consider the hundreds or more electronic resources (journals) that are delivered on different platforms by different vendors. Each resource has its own query structure, data field names, and layout of information on the computer screen (Serotkin et al 2005). There is little or no consistency between each of the resources and even knowledgeable experienced librarians often become frustrated with their search experiences. Libraries typically list these resources on their Web site (often in alphabetical order by product name). Many users have great difficulty in deciding what electronic resources to include in their searching.

And users may assume that by searching a particular database they are including the "XYZ" journal when, in fact, that particular journal is not included in the aggregated group of journals (called a database in library land).

Searching for information contained in journal articles is very difficult for many people. Most people do not consider starting at the library Web site to link to eJournals (only 15 percent according to the OCLC Perceptions report 2005). Most people learn about electronic information sources using a Web search engine followed by links from other Web sites, the news media, and online news. Interestingly, people will check with a friend, relative, coworker, teacher or post a query using instant messaging before checking with a librarian.

All of these problems leave an individual searching for information in a very frustrating position. It is also important to recognize that when people are searching they do not distinguish between different kinds of digital resources, viewing the library's catalog, abstracting services, eJournals, digital libraries, and Internet search engines as variations on a theme (Makri et al 2007).

An analysis of actual searching behavior suggests:

- *Horizontal information seeking.* People will view one or two pages from a Web site and then "bounce" out, most likely never to return.
- *Navigation.* People using digital libraries can spend as much time finding their way as they do actually viewing the content itself.
- *Viewing.* Rather than reading content on the Web site, users are "power browsing" through titles, abstracts and other summary information

with the result that they spend only four to eight minutes at an eJournal or eResource site.

- *Stockpiling behavior.* Users are quick to download content but there is as yet no research that has determined how much of this downloaded content is actually read or used in some manner.
- *Trust.* Users seem to rely on the reputation of the brand, e.g., Google, or the name of the journal itself, e.g., *Nature*, to determine whether content will be downloaded (Rowlands et al 2008).

Some digital libraries have developed query tools that retrieve non-textual materials. For example, a content-based image retrieval system can be created using computer software by categorizing images in terms of color, shape and texture (Wang and Liu 2008). Image indexing can provide access to images based on attributes of the image and can also provide access to useful groupings of images. Interestingly, this latter feature allows the user to select a display of random images and the user can then select one and the system will retrieve other similar images.

Some of the challenges associated with providing access to the visual materials include:

- Images often contain information useful to people from many disciplines
- The same image will likely have different meaning to different people
- The image is likely to be used for unanticipated reasons
- Images typically do not carry information about its creator and the context at the time of creation (Matusiak 2006).

Similar content-based query systems have been developed for audio and video files.

The Principle of Least Effort

The principle states that most people, even academic scholars and scientists, will choose easily available information sources – even if the source is of low quality. Further, people tend to be satisfied with whatever can be found easily in preference to tracking down high quality sources that would require a greater expenditure of effort.

The principle of least effort, sometimes called the 'principle of information seeking parsimony,' is also known as Zipf's Law of Least Effort that states:

> "Each individual will choose the option to obtain information that involves the least effort" (Zipf 1949).

The reality is that people tend to choose perceived ease of access over quality of content. And people will "satisfice" – a word first coined by Herb Simon to indicate that individuals will set modest goals and then stop searching when these goals are reached.

Evidence for the validity of this principle is substantial and covers many decades of study. Victor Rosenberg (1967) found in his investigation of information seeking behavior that the guiding principle for the design of any information system should be the system's ease of use rather than the amount or quality of information provided. Thomas Gerstberger and Thomas Allen (1967) arrived at a similar conclusion in their study of engineers and noted that there was a direct relationship between the perceived accessibility of an information channel and several objective measures of use. The observed behavior of engineers was to minimize the effort involved to gain access to information.

John Salasin and Toby Cedar (1985) in their study of 1,666 mental health practitioners, researchers and policymakers found that an information source was chosen based on the perceived ease of use rather than other criteria. And Herbert Poole (1985) noted that 43 out of 51 studies that focused on the information behavior of scientists demonstrate the principle of least effort.

Earlier, William Paisley (1968) noted that the level of frustration in using libraries is high for most people and that you "are conditioned to feeling that the library is a place where you almost have to drag something out of."

Thomas Mann (1993) has challenged the library profession when he observed that it was time to stop blaming library users for being 'lazy':

> Ironically, disregarding the Principle of Least Effort is itself a result of the same principle at work: it is easier for many library managers and information scientists to concentrate on "hard" problems of technology than to do the difficult library research on "soft" human behavior.

The implications of this principle are serious indeed and have been ignored by the library profession for far too long! It is time to focus on usability of the library physical and virtual collections and the tools used to gain access to these resources. Hoping that library users will recognize that the library contains quality resources and start using the library in increasing numbers is simply not going to happen.

Distributed Information Discovery

For many years, the hope was that a federated search engine would simplify the search process for the user. Since there is no local index to the contents of various databases, the search request is sent (in a unique properly formatted manner) to each library or database. The results are then returned (hopefully with the duplicate records deleted) and presented to the user. Federated searches can take from 15 seconds to as long as a minute or more (Chen 2006). This is clearly unacceptable given the speed with which Google performs and returns searches (tenths of a second).

In almost every case, the resulting display of a large amount of information was simply too confusing for the user and so users started avoiding the federated search tools provided by libraries.

Harvesting Metadata

A digital library can use the Open Archives Initiative Protocol for Metadata Harvesting (OAI-PMH) to export and import metadata from other digital libraries. OAI-PMH can export and/or import metadata about the digital collections in other digital libraries, archives or museums or the library may allow the export of metadata about the library's digital collection. Optionally, a copy of the digital objects in one library can be copied to another digital library. Item-level metadata is moved with each digital object that is also moved (Arms et al 2003).

A digital library can add value to its collections by providing the user with the ability to search metadata about other digital collections and objects that will complement the local library's digital resources. Consider a library that has a sizable collection of photographs, documents and diaries of soldiers who fought in the Battle of Gettysburg. If the library developed relationships with other libraries, museums, state historical societies and other similar organizations who had large or small Gettysburg-related digital content and was able to harvest the associated metadata (and perhaps harvest the digital objects themselves), the experience for the user of the digital library would be significantly enriched.

The challenge for the digital library is how to incorporate this influx of available metadata and/or digital objects so that the overall user experience is significantly improved and enhanced. In addition, the incoming data will be in an XML metadata format such as Dublin Core and will need to be integrated in a still largely MARC-centric library world. How should a library deal with the need to download, convert and manage metadata records from other digital sources is unexplored territory for almost all libraries. The real challenge is developing a crosswalk for metadata in one format to another format while dealing with issues such as lack of consistency in what data is placed in what field. While MARC provides a number of fields to represent "author" plus some contextual information, Dublin Core provides a single field for author field (with no contextual information).

In addition to being a consumer and creator of metadata (MARC records), digital libraries are moving to also being a distributor of metadata in a decentralized model.

Usability

As more services and functionality are added to a library's Web site, the more important usability becomes. Similarly, the library's online catalog – as the primary finding tool for library resources – continues to play a vital role in the lives of both library staff and library customers. The interaction between an individual and an automated system is called an interface. A useful definition of usability states that:

> The usability of an interface is a measure of the effectiveness, efficiency and satisfaction with which specified users can achieve specified goals in a particular environment with that interface (ISO 1999).

Jacob Nielsen (1995) suggests that there are five attributes of a usable interface and these include:

- It is easy to learn – Can users accomplish basic tasks the first time they use the site?
- It is efficient to use – How quickly can users perform basic tasks?
- It is easy to remember – When users return to a Web site, how quickly can they reestablish proficiency?
- It causes few errors – How many and how severe are the errors users make that are caused by the user interface? The user may make errors independent of the user interface.
- It is pleasant to use – Is the total experience pleasant or one the user leaves quickly?

The user's success with a particular user interface is predicated upon three primary factors:

- The amount of and accuracy of information
- The choice of indexes and the vocabulary selected for a specific search request
- The difficulty/friendliness in learning to use the user interface itself.

Site level usability includes information architecture, navigation and search; linking strategy, overall writing style; page templates, layout and site design standards; use of common icons, clarity of headlines and avoidance of jargon. For more specific suggests see the "10 Usability Tips" sidebar.

The density of information on most Web sites is quite high which essentially decreases the "findability" of information. Peter Morville (2005) suggests that "findability" is:

- The quality of being locatable or navigable
- The degree to which a particular object is easy to discover or locate
- The degree to which a system or environment supports navigation and retrieval.

Increasingly the Web that is emerging is social, mobile, real time, involves multimedia and is open.

Security

Clearly the security and integrity of all of the content contained within an automated system or a digital library must be protected and ensured. While a discussion of all of the threats to an automated system are beyond the scope of this book it's safe to say that adequate safeguards must be in place in the form of firewalls (hardware and software) to ensure that unauthorized individuals (sometimes known as hackers) are prevented from gaining entrance to the system and wreaking havoc.

Other Issues

Most users would like for the digital library to call their attention to content that might be important to the task at hand. You only have to think of the value of Amazon's recommendation system (it sells more items) to imagine the value in a library setting. Recommender systems built upon the past actions of others who have used the digital library have the potential for significantly enhancing the usefulness and utility of an online catalog. Thus, it is incumbent on any digital library system to incorporate the results on an analysis of the prior transactions - if this analysis occurs regularly and without the intervention of the library so much the better (Bearman 2007).

Libraries also have access to information about how frequently an item in its collection has been borrowed. This borrowing frequency data should be incorporated into all integrated library system ranked order display. Similarly, if a group of items were retrieved as a result of a search, and certain items were examined in greater detail by many of the searchers, these items should have greater visibility when retrieved again.

Summary

The search for information has radically changed over the course of the last twenty years. Google has become the standard both on the basis that they control the largest segment of all searching and that users are now expecting a similar search experience when using other services – including library Web sites and online catalogs. The end result is disintermediation (loosely understood and defined as "cutting out the middle man") so that the library is now on the outside looking in at the information seeking frenzy. Clearly discovery is happening elsewhere!

The challenge for any digital library is to make sure that the total customer experience, including the search for specific information, is easy to learn and provides real value to the customer. One of the ways a digital library can provide real value to its customers is by providing navigation tools that both display the search results but also suggest other ways of viewing the retrieved information and exploring other subsets of information. This is done by providing navigation aids that allows the user to browse in the information using a time line, perhaps a geographic basis using maps, providing links to other important related information, and so forth. The goal is to move beyond a text-oriented digital interface to one that encourages exploration in new and creative ways.

Survival Guide Tips

Finding your way in an emergency situation so that you are more likely to be rescued will only increase the likelihood of survival. Having a map and compass (and perhaps a GPS) would obviously be a big help in any survival situation. The most important part of using a map is orienting it to the surrounding area so that you truly know where you are and where you would like to go. And the compass or GPS allows you to keep on course.

- Recognize that for almost everyone when people think of information they think Google! The library is not in the information business.

- Convenience and speed trumps everything – quality of resources, friendly service, or ...

- Google and other easy-to-use Web sites are raising the bar of user expectations. The library must identify how it will stand out from the crowd while at the same time look and function more like search engines.

Survival Guide Tips - continued

- Enhanced content (table of contents, book jacket information, index terms, summary, reviews, and so forth) assist users in evaluating resources.

- The usability of the physical and virtual library will have the greatest impact on people liking it and returning again-and-again.

- Harvesting metadata from other digital libraries with content of interest is an important first step in creating a compelling digital library. The second step is focusing on creating a compelling and easy-to-use Web site that provides context.

- The future for any library is to clearly understand how a customer derives value from using your library. Then the library must change the way it delivers services so that the customer value proposition is the only perspective in determining how services are delivered.

10 Usability Tips

1. Forget the "Three-Click Rule" (if someone can't find what they are looking for within three clicks they are likely to then leave the Web site) and focus on ease of use.
2. Enable content skimming by using an F-shaped pattern. Users scan across and down a bit, and then down – the F-shaped pattern. Thus, don't locate important information in the lower right portion of the screen.
3. Speed up your Web site so users don't need to wait. More than a 2 second delay means reduced clicks and reduced user satisfaction.
4. Make your content easily readable and remember that most users read only 28% of available text. So less is more!
5. Don't worry about "The Fold" and vertical scrolling. Less content above the fold encourages scrolling.
6. Place important content on the left side of a Web page. Eyeballs are on the left side of the page about 69% of the time.
7. White space of text affects readability. Have good contrast between the text and the background and reduce the amount of text.
8. Small details make a huge difference. Replacing the cryptic 404 error with a polite two-sentence message will improve usage of a Web site.
9. Don't rely on search as a crutch for bad navigation.
10. Your home page isn't as important as you think.

Adapted from Chapman 2010.

Chapter 7

Using Information

"One of the effects of living with electric information
is that we live habitually in a state of information
overload. There's always more than you can cope with."

Marshall McLuhan

G iven the rapid advances and adoption of information technology by people, it is not surprising that people are now more comfortable with the use of digital information at home, work and play. Increasingly the physical library is being disintermediated as information providers such as eJournal publishers, eResource content aggregators, Google Books and others market their products directly to the end user.

Desktop Access

Clearly, as the use of electronic resources continues to increase year after year, the only logical conclusion is that people prefer desktop access from their home or office to gain access to these resources. The customer is able to discover, locate and download one or more journal articles or other electronic resources without the need to physically travel to the library. And they are also able to avoid taking the time to locate the desired print resource and making photocopies of the desired

article(s) in the library. Convenience trumps
everything!

Mobile Access

Given that mobile devices are no longer considered as a
technology but rather as a core behavior their
proliferation should not be surprising. About 5 billion
people will have a mobile phone by the end of 2011.
Thus, we have gone way beyond the tipping point in
terms of adoption of mobile devices. It should not be
surprising that people expect Internet access from these
devices. They are also downloading and reading eBooks
on their hand-held mobile devices. Almost everyone is
using mobile as a communications platform to place and
receive calls, emails, texts, pictures, videos and Internet
Web sites. For some, their mobile devices (especially
smart phones) have replaced their desktop computer.
The implication of mobile access for a library is to do
one thing really well.

eBooks & eBook Readers

Books are big business around the world. In 2009,
people spent US $108 billion on all types and sizes of
books. So it is not surprising that eBooks are becoming
more popular every year.

eBooks are electronic books. They are books in digital
format that are read with the assistance of an electronic
device such as an eReader, computer (desktop, laptop,
iPad) or cell phone. The goal for an eBook reader is to
emulate the basic characteristics of the traditional
printed book while leveraging information technology
and the Internet to make the process easy to use. It is
interesting to note that "way" back in 2001, Forrester

Research suggested, "eBooks are likely to be an e-failure." Well, the times have clearly changed.

There are a number of different eBook file formats. These file formats can be identified by their file type extensions. Some of the most common eBook file formats include .azw (Kindle eBook format), .PDF, .ePUB, and .pdb (known as e-reader). See the sidebar for more information about this topic.

ePUB is the format most eBooks use and it is an extensible markup language similar to HTML. The goal of ePUB, a standard of the International Digital Publishing Forum, is to allow the transfer of information from one device to another reader. The ePUB standard is composed of three open standards:

- The Open Publication Structure (OPS) – defines the formatting of the content
- The Open Packaging Format (OPF) – describes the structure of the ePUB file in XML
- The Open Container Format (OCF) – collects all files into a single file system entity.

The ePUB text adapts to the user's eReader or other device. Text can be redrawn on the screen to make it bigger or smaller. However, an ePUB book does not have static page numbers (which are important to most academic users). In addition, publishers can lock down content using a Digital Rights Management system, which rescinds the benefits of ePUB (Polanka 2011).

eBook File Formats

Extension	Format	Governing Organization	DRM
.azw	Kindle	Amazon proprietary	Yes
.djvu	Pronounced "déjà vu" is a digital document format for high resolution images	Caminova proprietary	Yes
.epub	epub	International Digital Publishing Forum	Yes
.html	Hypertext Markup Language	World Wide Web Consortium	No
.lit	Literate	Microsoft proprietary	Yes
.lrf, .lrx	Broadband eBooks	Sony proprietary	Yes
.mobi	Mobipocket ebook	Mobipocket proprietary	Yes
.opf	Open Packaging Format – part of the epub ebook specification	IDPF proprietary	Yes
.pdb	Program Database – eReader	Palm Media proprietary	Yes
.pdf	Portable Document Format	Adobe	Yes
.rtf	Rich Text Format	Microsoft proprietary	No
.tr3	TomeRaider ebook File	TomeRaider	Yes
.txt	Text File	International Standards Organization	No
.xeb	A Markup Language - popular format for Chinese eBooks	Founder Electronics	Yes

The popularity of eBooks is undeniable as the Association of American Publishers reported that sales had risen to $313 million in 2009, exceeding sales of audio books (AAP 2010). And in 2010 eBooks sales were $966 million. Some have suggested that eBook sales will jump to almost $3 billion by 2015. eBook sales are increasing for almost every publisher although the availability of core reading list materials (monographs and textbooks) that are central to most academic programs and intended for intensive use by students have been slow to develop. Today, students and faculty members are split on the potential use of eBooks as a substitute for textbooks.

- A third would prefer print only
- A third would like a hybrid of print and electronic resources
- And the final third seek all electronic resources.

The forecast for the eBook market is quite bullish and reflects the shift to digital information that is currently under way. A British report suggested that by the year 2020, 40 percent of the UK research monographs would only be available in electronic format and a further 50 percent would be produced in both digital and print (British Library 2005).

Another study of 1,200 respondents indicated that 40 percent of eReader owners revealed that they read more eBooks than they previously did reading pBooks (Fowler and Baca 2010).

However, the picture from the perspective of the consumer is total confusion. Most publishers use a multiplicity of booksellers in order to maximize revenues. Depending upon the title, where the consumer buys the eBook will have a significant impact on the price paid. If the eBook is purchased then the price can vary from about $8 to as much as $20, depending on the eReader and eBook chosen. In addition, it is possible, in some cases, to rent an eBook for 14 to 60 days for $5 to $15.

It is important to remember that the eBook reader is designed for the individual and not for libraries. In an ideal world, the library would provide eBooks that were readable on any platform so that the library could distribute eBooks on multiple devices and it would also be able to loan eBooks to users on their own devices.

There are a number of eBook readers that are currently available. Some of the leading ones include:

Alex

The Alex e-reader, from Spring Design, is slim, trim and easy to use. It features a 6-inch reader display screen plus a 3.5-inch color touch screen smartphone-like Web browser. A progress slide bar on the color screen allows the user to jump to a later or earlier page with the touch of a finger. The price of an Alex is $299.

eDGe

The eDGe, developed by enTourage, is a dual-screen eReader (using E Ink technology) with a tablet-style netbook. The eReader screen is 9.7 inches and the tablet screen is 10.1 inches in size. The device has a dual-hinge design. The tablet functionality comes with web browsing using the built in Wi-Fi, audio/video record and playback, an email function and contacts list, a calculator, an alarm clock, and a library function to manage your books and files. Not surprisingly, the eDGe is a bit on the pricey side - $499 retail. enTourage calls their device the "dualbook."

Kindle

Amazon.com sells the Kindle and users can purchase eBooks on their Web site. The eBooks are sold as a Digital Rights Management (DRM) solution so that Amazon can control how the downloaded content is used and the eBook can only be read by the Kindle. The Kindle is unable to render color as it uses e-ink technology, which provides 16 shades of gray. It also does not display photographs, diagrams and tables very well, which are typically very important in the academic environment.

Three versions of the Kindle are available today: the Kindle 3 comes with a 6-inch screen and Wi-Fi ($139); the Kindle 3 with 3G and Wi-Fi also has a 6-inch screen ($189); and the Kindle DX that has a 9.7-inch screen and supports native PDF files and 3G wireless ($379).

Amazon.com in the US has more than 750,000 eBooks that can be downloaded to only one eBook reader, the Kindle. Yet the popularity of the Kindle is demonstrated by the fact that Amazon sold seven million in 2010 and expects to sell twelve million in 2011. Amazon has about 19 percent of the pBook marketplace but some estimate that it has over 90 percent of the eBook marketplace! The Kindle is popular due to its:

- *Smooth user interface design.* It is light, easy to hold, and provides a simple and intuitive user interface.
- *Content downloads easily.* The speed and simplicity of the download process is inspiring. In less than a minute you can purchase, download and start reading a book.
- *Cross*-device content delivery. Through the use of Kindle Reader apps, you can use your laptop, desktop, iPhone, iPad, Android and other devices to access Kindle eBooks.
- *Synching.* The Kindle remembers where you left off reading your book automatically. Pretty nifty.
- *Public domain titles.* It is possible to download free public domain eBooks from such sites as Project Gutenberg.

The downside of the Kindle is that while you can now share an eBook for 14 days, the sharing is only with another Kindle or Kindle app user (and while the book is out on loan, you are unable to read it). While many decry the fact that the library is unable to provide access to the Amazon eBooks in the way the library might like, the reality is that as the market leader, Amazon's business model is not serving libraries but rather in selling copies of eBooks to its customers. Thus, Amazon has developed and is controlling a closed proprietary platform. Amazon is only interested in seeing its revenues and profits grow – not serving the library marketplace.

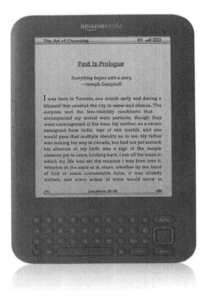

Kindle

Kobo

The Kobo, from Borders, allows readers to choose from five font sizes and either a serif or sans serif typeface. However, it lacks Wi-Fi and 3G capabilities so books must be downloaded first to a computer and then moved to the reader. The Kobo screen is fairly dull (based on comments from several reviews) and turning pages is slow. The price of a Kobo is $130.

Libre

The Libre eBook Reader Pro, developed by Aluratek, is a lightweight reader that comes with MP3 capabilities. This low priced reader ($100) has a dull display and the characters do not appear to be very crisp.

Nook

Barnes & Noble sells three versions of the Nook: Nook Wi-Fi, Nook 3G Wi-Fi, and the Nook Color. Its built-in Wi-Fi allows the user to connect automatically to Barnes & Noble to quickly purchase and download eBooks, newspapers and periodicals. Similar in terms of ergonomics and price to the Kindle, the Nook offers more choice in terms of what can be downloaded. The Nook also provides a user-replaceable battery and a memory expansion slot. The price is $149 for the Nook Wi-Fi.

Barnes & Noble has established a program called LendMe that allows a user to lend an eBook for 14 days to another individual. The user notifies Barnes & Noble of their desire to lend a title to someone, Barnes & Noble notifies the individual and they have 7 days to accept the download. Note that during the 7 days (and the 14 days that follow if the lend is accepted) the title is not available to the original purchaser to read.

Nook

Novel

The Pandigital Novel reader is an Android-powered device with a bright high-resolution 7-inch color touch screen, Wi-Fi and a Web browser. Customers can download eBooks from Barnes & Noble, read any ePUB or PDF file. The Novel is similar to an iPad and can run most Android apps. The Novels' touch screen is glass and thus highly reflective, fragile and hard to read in direct sunlight. The price of a Novel is $169.

Sony Reader

Sony has three versions of its reader: the Pocket Reader Edition, the Touch Reader Edition, and the Daily Reader Edition. Each has different functionality and a price point to match. The Pocket Reader is the least expensive ($199) and has a 5-inch display. The Touch Reader with its 6-inch anti-glare touch screen that lets the reader turn pages and navigate with a swipe of a finger has a retail price of $299. The Daily Reader Edition at $399 has a larger 7-inch screen and a built-in 3G wireless coverage provided by AT&T. It is possible to make freehand notes and highlight text. Books are quickly downloaded from a variety of sources using a variety of formats. The readers will also play audio files. The price is $229.

eBook Reader Comparison Chart

Feature	Alex	eDGe	Kindle	Kobo	Libre	Nook	Novel	Sony
Price	$299	$499	$189 for the 3G	$130	$170	$149 for Wi-Fi	$169	$229
Weight	16 oz.	3 lbs.	8.7 oz.	8 oz.	7.6 oz.	11.6 oz.	16 oz.	7.6 oz.
Device size	4.7 x 8.9 x .6 inch	8.3 x 10.8 x 1 inch	4.8 x 7.5 x .33 inch	4.7 x 7.2 x .4 inch	4.3 x 6.0 x .6 inch	4.9 x 7.7 x .5 inch	5.5 x 7.5 x .5 inch	4.7 x 6.6 x .4 inch
Device type	E Ink , LED back-lit touch scrn	E Ink	E Ink	E Ink	TFT - Thin film tran-sistor	E Ink	LED backlit color touch screen	E Ink
Screen size	7 in. & 3.5 in.	9.7 in. Read-er & 10.1 inch Tab-let	6 in.	6 in.	5 in.	6 in.	7 in.	6 in.
Internal storage	256 MB	3 GB	3 GB	1 GB	117 MB	1.3 GB	1 GB	2 GB
Conn-ections	USB, Wi-Fi	USB, Wi-Fi	USB, 3G, Wi-Fi	USB, Blue-tooth	USB	USB, Wi-Fi	USB, Wi-Fi	USB, Wi-Fi

Mobile Devices & Apps

In addition to the eBook readers, many vendors have developed applications or apps that can be downloaded so that a mobile device such as an iPhone, iPad, Literati, and Android can be used to read a book. It is no longer "strange" to see someone looking at their mobile device for extended periods of time as they read. These mobile devices are being used more hours per day every year.

Apple announced that they had sold 1.5 million eBooks during the first month that the iPad was sold (1 million iPads were sold the first month). Some industry pundits are suggesting that the eReader will disappear over time as more and more people embrace the iPad and other tablet-like devices.

There are a wide variety of eBook apps that can be downloaded to most mobile devices. The costs of these apps range from zero to a few dollars. There are several apps for reading books, magazines, newspapers, blogs, and so forth.

eBooks and Libraries

As with eJournals, libraries do not purchase eBooks but rather they are licensed. So the license fees must be considered as an ongoing expense that will not disappear. This has important budgetary implications since as time goes on, libraries will have less flexibility to adjust their purchasing of new materials. Rather, they will find themselves "locked in" to the need to pay the yearly licensing fee to gain access to electronic content – be they journal articles or eBooks. Cancel the subscription and the eBooks are gone.

The availability of eBooks has complicated things for libraries since library users want traditional services and they also want access to digital content as well. Thus, libraries are being confronted with the challenge of how to lend eBooks. Some libraries want to purchase eBook readers and loan them to patrons. Others only want to provide access to an eBook provider on behalf of their customers. This is particularly challenging given the variety of business models and the many eBook readers that are available in the marketplace. In some ways, this is analogous to playing "pin the tail on the donkey" while blindfolded and having many participants tugging you in different directions at the same time. Getting an eBook from a library is often a confusing and multistep process that involves visits to three or more Web sites. In fact, the confusion is so prevalent that many libraries have created tutorials on the process of downloading an eBook.

Some business models focus on "one user at a time" while other business models cater to multiple/ simultaneous users so the same material can be accessed at the same time by multiple people – regardless of their location. Some publishers prefer to sell their eBooks directly to the end user while others offer their eBooks though online stores such as Amazon, Barnes & Noble, Sony, AppleA, Google, OverDrive, ProQuest and others.

The popularity of eBooks cannot be denied. OverDrive, a vendor who provides eBooks for libraries, announced that during 2010, 15 million digital titles were checked out, 6.6 million minutes of spoken audio was downloaded and that OverDrive provides access to 400,000 eBook, audiobook, music and video titles. Yet, despite this success, the reality is that using the

OverDrive service is complicated and very hard to use. Many library users find the difficulties of incompatible media formats – a Microsoft .wma audiobook format will not work on a Mac – difficult to overcome so they give up in frustration. Even worse, if a user attempts to download an ebook using OverDrive but the book is already checked out to another library customer, then they can't complete the download. It sure would be nice if ebook readers and the wide variety of file formats played well with each other would it not?

Students like the searching function available in an ebook reader as well as the anytime/anywhere access. They also like being able to copy and paste text into a word processing document. Rather than reading an ebook in its entirety, students prefer to scan and browse content. One big frustration for many users is the inability to annotate and make notes within the eBook (Hernon 2007).

A study of ebook readers in higher education found three major problems: 1) limitations in the design of the device so that the user had problems with searching, annotation and movement within the eBook itself; 2) functional limitations with an electronic device that prevents having more than one text item open simultaneously, the lack of visual clues as to the place (front, middle or back) within the eBook, and the difficultly in navigating between texts quickly; and 3) the lack of flexibility in the device itself that prevents the print or exchange of eBooks or downloading of information into a desktop or laptop computer (Spiro and Henry 2010). Almost everyone would agree that none of the existing eBook readers provides an acceptable means of making, keeping and moving annotations in the eBook environment.

For libraries, DRM (Digital Rights Management) is the biggest issue. DRM essentially says that you own the right to read the eBook but it is not yours to lend, sell or give away. The Digital Millennium Copyright Act prohibits any circumvention of DRM and includes no exceptions for libraries. This Copyright Act eliminated the "First Sale" Doctrine that allows libraries to purchase and then lend their materials. Libraries would prefer to purchase eBooks with no DRM so that the library can purchase for whatever platform (eBook reader) is desired.

The library must also track what eBooks they have purchased and loaded on what devices. They must also decide on what eBook reader(s) to purchase and loan to customers. It is possible to use a commercial product such as Adobe Content Server to circulate eBooks (even place limits of one-copy-at-a-time) rather than relying on such vendors as OverDrive. This is important as the eBook marketplace is in a state of flux. eBooks are yet another example of how disintermediation is negatively impacting libraries. In fact, OverDrive noted that "Library eBook catalogs and budgets are limited and incapable of meeting consumer demand for titles in print or eBook formats" (2010).

Sources of eBooks

Commercial Vendors

eBooks.Com
BooksOnBoard.Com
KoboBooks.Com
eLibrary.Net
eBook.Com
Borders.Com

BarnesAndNoble.Com
eReader.Com
eBookStore.Sony.Com
MobiPocket.Com/en/Books
Google.Com/eBooks
Baen Books

Library Vendors

WorldLibrary.Net
eblib.Net
EBSCO.Com
ProQuest.Com (NetLibrary)
Swets.Com
Muse.Jhu.Edu
Jstor.Org

Free eBooks

FreeBookSpot.Biz
4eBooks.Org
Free-eBooks.Net
ManyBooks.Net
GetFreeEbooks.Com
FreeComputerBooks.Com
FreeTechBooks.Com
Scribd.Com
Globusz.Com
KnowFree.Net
OnlineFreeBooks.Net
MemoWare.Com
BluePortal.Org
OnlineComputerBooks.Com
SnipFiles.Com
BookYards.Com
AskSam.Com

EBookLobby.Com
Gutenberg.Org
FeedBooks.Com
Online Books Page
(www.Digital.Library.UPenn.Edu/Books/

Sharing eBooks

ebookFling.Com offers eBook sharing for free

eBook Search Engine

InkMess.Com searches for online sources for free
eBooks

Tip!

Check out this Web site in order
to download almost 500 classic books
in eBook format along with their
associated MARC cataloging records.
http://www.clicweb.org/e_discover/e_discoverhome.html
The eBooks are loaded into the library's online catalog
obviating the need to go to another Web site.

Summary

While existing eBook readers offer many exciting features, they also carry a corresponding set of functional frustrations for the user of these devices. The biggest benefit of eBooks is the quick (you can download 24/7) access to the content within the book. The biggest drawback for many people is that they do not want to read content, especially scholarly content, on a computer screen. However, the increasing popularity of eBook readers and the increasing sales of eBooks indicate that there is a major shift occurring as people move to the convenience of using the eBook reader in a variety of settings.

From all of the above it is possible to suggest that:

- More books will be appearing in the eBook format
- The number of eReader devices will continue to grow
- In time the eReader may fall out of favor due to the increasing popularity of the iPad and its competitors
- The emergence of a single eBook publishing standard will not likely happen anytime soon (if ever)
- The total amount of reading that people are doing appears to remain relatively constant – it's just that the reading is taking place using different mediums – computer screens, iPads, mobile devices and eBook readers
- Libraries will continue to struggle to provide access to eBooks given the continuing demand of publishers to utilize DRM technology (Duncan 2010).

Survival Guide Tips

In any survival situation where the temperatures may drop to near or below freezing, the ability to build and maintain a fire can be the difference between life and death. Thus, having a set of matches (especially if there are treated to resist moisture) can make a real difference and improve your chances of surviving.

- Providing desktop access to electronic resources for the library's customers is crucial (even if few people think "library" when they are doing so).

- Providing access to electronic resources for each customer's mobile device is no longer an option – it's mandatory (at least from the customer's perspective). Do you provide an app that can be downloaded to accomplish this?

- eBooks are taking on an increasingly important role in the lives of a library's customers. Is your library providing a set of eBooks that customers can easily download? Are you eBook reader device independent?

- Is your library positioned so that it can provide 24/7 access to electronic resources – regardless of format?

Libraries Are So Screwed

Eli Neiburger, Associate Director of the Ann Arbor District Library, gave a provocative talk during the Library Journal/School Library Journal virtual conference on Ebooks: Libraries at the Tipping Point (September 2010). The "official" title of Eli's presentation was *Libraries at the Tipping Point: How eBooks Impact Libraries*. The "unofficial" title was *Libraries Are So Screwed*.

You can listen to Eli's presentation at YouTube http://www.youtube.com/watch?v=KqAwj5ssU2c&feature= player_embedded

You can download his PowerPoint presentation at http://www.slideshare.net/we2aam/ebooks-impact

In summary, Eli's thesis is the following:

"Libraries are screwed, because we are invested in the codex, and the codex has become outmoded. It's not just a change of text delivery format, it's a move away from content that is ownable and shareable, and that's a problem when your organization is in the business of owning and sharing content."

"The brand of libraries is the book temple. Come to the book temple and get yourself some books. Avid library users know that there's more to it, but...our values and our operation parameters and even our physical facilities are all built around the codex. If [the eBook] is the future of text distribution, then we're really screwed, because we are unlikely to ever have the access to these markets and the flexibility with our purchases that we currently have with the codex market."

"The real problem is that the value of library collections is rooted in the worth of a local copy. The localness of something loses most of its embodied value when you can retrieve information from Australia in 300 milliseconds. Who cares if it's local or not? I have it immediately. The notion of a copy loses most of its embodied value when there's no longer a difference between transmission and duplication. When you're dealing with digital objects, to transmit it is to duplicate it. If you know where it is, you'll always have it. There are already more cell phones in the world than there are toilets, and in this century most humans are going to have persistent Internet access in their pocket. In an internetworked world, when you can download anything from anywhere, the idea of having a local copy only makes sense to a hoarder."

"There may not always be new material made available in formats that libraries can purchase. This has already started – we had our first request this past week for an item that is not available in print, it's only available on the Kindle. There's no way that we can buy it."

"No digital native is going to get excited about waiting to receive a digital object, and what's the sense in making someone give something back to you when you still have it even after you gave it to them? Finally, the user experiences available to people who choose not to bother trying to use the library will only provide increasingly appealing value, which puts us in the situation where all this is happening as taxpayers are having to decide what municipal services they can live without. We are so screwed."

Eli's presentation really gives one pause and raises some real important issues that every library needs to address as we move into the digital library arena.

Chapter 8

So You Want to Digitize

> 'The biggest problem is not
> to let people accept new ideas,
> but to let them forget the old ones.'
>
> John Maynard Keynes

Prior to embarking on a journey to create a digital library, the library director and the library management team should explicitly address six important questions. These questions are:

- **Why?** Why is there a need for a digital library? What information needs will be met and for whom?

- **What?** What kind of data will be accessible and available in the digital library? What is unique about the digital content that will attract users? What data formats will be supported – textual, images, audio, video and so forth? What level of metadata and other finding aids will be provided?

- **Who?** Who is going to be responsible for the digital library? Who will be digitizing some of the existing materials in the library's collections? Who will determine what "born digital" content will be added and maintained in the digital library? Do the designated staff members have the requisite skills and competencies today? Who will create and enhance the user interface for the digital library? Equally important is to ask who the digital library's potential customers are. What type of individuals does the customer audience include? Will the digital library enable the library to reach new audiences for the digital surrogates?

- **How?** How will the data be stored and manipulated using what tools? How will users search for the digital content beyond "simple" text searching? How will users discover all of the digital resources (and their associated limitations) when using the digital library?

- **Where?** Where will the digital content associated with the digital library be located? Will the library, an IT department or an outside organization in the cloud be responsible for the maintenance of the hardware and software supporting the digital library?

- **When?** When will the digital library go live? How often is additional digital content added to the library? (Abdullah and Zainab 2008).

Digital images are electronic "snapshots" that result from scanning documents, photographs, manuscripts, printed texts, artwork and a wide range of other materials. The process of creating digital images is called digitization.

It is important to create digital masters that have high enough resolution to be useful over time and to reduce or eliminate the need to scan or digitize a work two or more times over a ten-year period. Digital files can be created to replace or reduce use of vulnerable deteriorating originals, provided the digital surrogate offers an accurate representation. A high-end digital master that is "purpose blind" should be created and it can be used to create derivatives that meet a variety of current and future needs. The quality of the original scan directly affects the quality, utility, and expense of derivatives that might be used for publication, image display or computer processing. Some have called derivatives access images.

The goal of digitization should be to safeguard the long-term value of the images and the investment in acquiring and producing them. Derivative images need to meet current user needs and technological capabilities. Avoid the problem that some libraries have experienced in that they based their digitization standards on prevailing technical constraints of monitors, printers, software, and the network only to discover that their image files do not lend themselves to reuse as the technology improves (which is constantly occurring).

The Basics

During the scanning process, the *digital image* is sampled and mapped as a grid of dots or picture elements (pixels). Each *pixel* is assigned a value (black, white, shades of gray or color), which is represented in binary code (ones and zeros). The binary digits (bits) are stored in a sequence by the computer. In some cases, an algorithm is used to reduce the size of the file while still preserving the content. This reduction process is called compression.

The *pixel dimensions* are the horizontal and vertical measurements of an image expressed in pixels. The pixel dimensions can be determined by multiplying the width and height by the number of pixels or *pixels per inch* (ppi) also referred to as *dots per inch* (dpi). For example, a 4" by 5" photograph that is scanned at 300 dpi has the pixel dimensions of 1,200 pixels (4" by 300 dpi) by 1,500 dpi (5" by 300 dpi).

When scanning with a camera, a different calculation is used. Consider a 12-megapixel camera whose horizontal width is 4,032. Dividing the 4,032 by 8.5 inches (for an 8.5 by 11 inch page size) provides a dpi of 474.

The ability to distinguish fine spatial detail is called resolution. The spatial frequency at which the digital image is sampled – the sampling frequency – is a good indicator of resolution. This is why dots per inch (dpi) or pixels per inch (ppi) are interchangeable terms that are used to express resolution for digital images. Generally, increasing the sampling frequency (increasing the dpi) helps to improve resolution.

Each bit depth or pixel can be defined using different methods. These include:

- The *bitonal image* of black and white is represented by 1 bit (one or zero)
- A *gray scale image* is composed of pixels represented by multiple bits of information (ranging from 2 to 8). At 8 bits, 256 (2^8) different tones can be assigned to each pixel
- A *color image* can be represented by a bit depth ranging from 8 to 24 bits or higher. A 24-bit pixel offers 16.7 million (2^{24}) color values.

The dynamic range is the tonal difference between the lightest light and the darkest dark of an image. The higher the dynamic range, the more potential shades that can be represented. Dynamic range describes a digital system's ability to reproduce tonal information and is most important for photographs and continuous-tone documents.

The material being scanned has different characteristics, which have implications when scanned. These characteristics include:

- *Text* – is characterized by regular relatively wide spacing between long thin strokes of relatively uniform width. Fonts may be serifs or sans serifs typeface.
- *Half tones* – are traditionally dark dots of varying size laid out on a regular spaced grid. A variation distributes the same size dot in pseudo-random order to achieve the different shades of gray.
- *Line art and engravings* – has relatively uniform width markings of long strokes.
- *Continuous tones* – have smooth variations between adjacent reflective values.

File size is calculated by multiplying the surface area of the document (width X height) to be scanned by the bit depth and the dpi[2]. The result is divided by 8 (8 bits make up 1 byte) to determine the file size. Since digital images often result in very large files, the number of bytes is usually represented in increments of 1,024. For example:

1 Kilobyte (KB)	1,024 bytes	Half a printed page
1 Megabyte (MB)	1,024 KB	The Bible
1 Gigabyte (GB)	1,024 MB	A section of library shelves
1 Terabyte (TB)	1,024 GB	Million-volume library
1 Petabyte (PB)	1,024 TB	Large scientific database
1 Exabyte (EB)	1,024 PB	1/4th of the world's disk production
1 Zettabyte (ZB)	1,024 EB	Total amount of global data in 2010

The size of the resulting file for each scanned image increases with the *square* of the resolution – *doubling the resolution quadruples the file size*. The following formula can be used to estimate the resulting file size when an item is being digitized.

$$\text{File size (in bytes)} = \frac{\text{Height x Width x bit-depth x dpi}^2}{8 \text{ bits per byte}}$$

Since the digital images can be quite large, taxing the computing and network capabilities of many organizations, *compression* is often used to reduce file size. All compression techniques use a mathematical algorithm to accomplish this task. There are standard and proprietary compression techniques and it is always better to use a standard-based technique. Many libraries and museums will not use a compression method to store the original digital image but may use a compressed file for other activities.

Compression schemes can be characterized as either:

- **Lossless** – abbreviates the binary code without discarding any information so that the image can be "decompressed" and it is a bit by bit match with the original
- **Lossy** – averages or discards the least significant information however it is difficult to detect the effects of lossy compression. JPEG is a file format that uses a lossy compression scheme.

File formats consist of the bits that comprise the digital image and the header information on how to read and interpret the file. File formats vary in terms of resolution, bit depth, color capabilities, and support for compression and metadata. See Figure 8-1 for more detailed information about file formats.

Figure 8-1. Common Image File Formats

Name	Ext.	Bit depth	Standard/ Proprietary	Compression	Color Mgmt	Web Support	Metadata Support
Flashpix	.fpx	8-bit grayscale; 24-bit color	Publicly available specification	Uncompressed Lossy: JPEG	PhotoYCC, NIF RGB	Plug-in	Set of labeled tags
GIF – Graphics Interchange Format	.gif	1-8 bit bitonal, grayscale or color	De facto standard	Lossless: LZW	Palette	Native	Free-text comment field
JP2-JPX/ JPEG 2000	.jp2, .jpx, .j2k, .j2c	1-38 bits, grayscale or color	ISO 15444	Uncompressed Lossless/ Lossy	Palette, YC_bC_r	Plug-in	Basic set of labeled tags
JPEG – Joint Photographic Expert Group	.jpeg , .jpg	8-bit grayscale; 24-bit color	ISO 10918	Lossy: JPEG Lossless	YC_bC_r	Native	Free-text comment field
PDF – Portable Document Format	.pdf	4-bit grayscale; 8-bit color	De facto standard	Uncompressed Lossless	RGB, YC_bC_r	Plug-in or ext. application	Basic set of labeled tags
PNG – Portable Network Graphics	.png	1-16 bit grayscale; 24 or 48-bit color	ISO 15948	Lossless	Palette	Native	Basic set of labeled tags + user defined tags
TIFF – Tagged Image File Format	.tif, .tiff	1-bit bitonal 4 or 8-bit grayscale; up to 64-bit color	De facto standard	Uncompressed Lossless	RGB, Palette, YC_bC_r	Plug-in or ext. application	Basic set of labeled tags

A majority of digitized documents are scanned and stored in TIFF files. However, there are many flavors of TIFF. Some TIFF flavors are:

- Uncompressed TIFF – A standard format for scanned images. An uncompressed TIFF file has the largest file size.
- TIFF G3 – International standard for faxes and multipage line-art documents. Only used for black-and-white documents.
- TIFF G4 – A lossless compressed archival file format for bitonal images that has the smallest file size of all the various options.
- TIFF Huffmann – A method for compressing bi-level data with the CCITT Group 3 ID facsimile compression schema.
- TIFF LZW – The Lempel-Ziv & Welch (LZW) algorithm is a lossless compression method that may be used for bitonal, gray scale, and color images. Savings in file size may be as much as 50 percent using this method.
- TIFF Zip – Zip compression is a lossless method effective for images that contain large areas of a single color.
- TIFF JPEG – As a lossy compression method, this is a JPEG file inside a TIFF file.

Based on all of the above information, a scanning decision tree provides recommended scanning levels as shown in Figure 8-2.

Figure 8-2. Scanning Decision Tree*

Issue		No Detail	Fine Detail	Extremely Fine Detail
Significant Color Content?	Yes	200 dpi Color JPEG	300 dpi Color JPEG	600 dpi Color JPEG
Continuous Tone or Halftone	Yes	200 dpi Gray scale JPEG	300 dpi Gray scale JPEG	600 dpi Color JPEG
Need to Retain Brightness Discrimination	Yes	200 dpi Gray scale JPEG	300 dpi Gray scale JPEG	600 dpi Gray scale JPEG
	No	300 dpi Binary Group 4	600 dpi Binary Group 4	1200 dpi Binary Group 4

* Adapted from Library of Congress 2006.

Audio and Video

There are two primary formats for audio files: a high-quality standard for music and a low-quality standard for voice. When digitizing sound, the frequency range in kHz determines the sampling rate. The sampling rate must be double the highest frequency that is to be captured. The music CD format stores 44,100 samples per second at 16 bits per sample on each of two audio tracks – clearly above what the average human can hear. Recording the sound rather than storing the text spoken requires 1,000 times as much storage space.

The following tables provide suggestions for the audio preservation master and presentation formats.

Audio Preservation Master

Level	Format	Sample Rate	Bit-depth	Usage Example
Minimum	WAV / AIFF	44,000	16	Audio from commercial CD
Special circumstances	WAV / AIFF	48,000	24	Human voice only, no music
Recommended	WAV / AIFF	96,000	24	Oral history recording with music or sounds from nature

Audio Presentation Format

Level	Format	Bit rate	Usage Example
Minimum	MP3	128 Kbps	Oral history without music
Recommended	MP3	192 Kbps	Most audio
Special	MP3	320 Kbps	High fidelity required

In the same way, the library will need to make decisions about what standard and format to use to digitize video files. More information about the audio and video file format options may be found in Figures 8-3 and 8-4.

Video Preservation Master

Level	Format	Encoding	Resolution	Sample Size	Data Rate
Recommended	MXF	Uncompressed YCbCr or JPEG2000 lossless	640 x 480	30 bit progressive scanning	30 Mbps
Acceptable	MXF	MPEG-4 AVC or DV	640 x 480	30 bit progressive scanning	30 Mbps

Video Derivative Copy

Level	Encoding	Resolution	Data Rate
Suggested	MPEG-4 AVC	320 x 240	256 – 600 Kbps

Figure 8-3 Audio File Formats

Format	Extension	Description	Meaning	Strengths/ Weaknesses
Audio Inter-change File	.aif, .aifc	.aifc has compressed samples	Developed by Apple, this is a non-compressed format that can't be streamed	High-quality flexible format
SUN Audio	.au, .snd		Typically used with Unix computers	Slow de-compression rates
MPEG-1 Layer 3	.mp3		Typical compression of 10:1. Samples at 32000, 44100 and 48000 Hz	Small file sizes with good quality output
PARIS – Profession al Audio Record-ing Integrat-ed System	.paf	Used with the Ensoniq PARIS digital audio editing system	Can contain 8, 16 or 24 bit	
Real Audio	.ra	Commonly used with the Web	Acceptable sound quality & uses 10:1 lossy com-pression	
Sound Designer II	.sdii	Commonly used on Macs (problems with PCs)	Defacto standard for file transfers	Large file sizes
IRCAM	.sf	Arbitrary sampling rate that uses 8 or 16 bit		

Figure 8-3 – continued

Format	Extension	Description	Meaning	Strengths/ Weaknesses
Wave	.wav	Windows media non-compressed format – used on Mac & the PC	Arbitrary sampling rate of 8, 16 or 32 bit	Large file sizes
Musical Instrument Digital Interface	.mid, .midi	A file that does not contain music but instructions about music events and objects	Defines codes for the start of a note, its pitch, its length, volume and so forth.	

Figure 8-4. Video File formats

Format	Extension	Description	Strengths/ Weaknesses
Moving Picture Experts Group	.mpg	MPEG-1 – Video CD MPEG-2 – DVD MPEG-4 – Multimedia on the Web MPEG-7 – Multimedia Content Description Interface	Good quality and low files sizes
Quick Time	.qt, .mov	Initially created for Macs, also on PCs. Has streaming capabilities	Excellent quality and file sizes can be large
Vivo	.viv	Played on VivoActive player	Poor quality due to high compression rates
Real Media	.rma	Proprietary streaming format	Requires RealMedia plug-in
Windows Media Player	.wma	Streaming format	Good quality

Scanners

An image scanner, often shortened to just scanner, is a device that optically scans images, text, handwriting or an object and converts it to a digital image. Scanners typically use a charge-coupled device as the image sensor. The charge-coupled device usually contains three rows of sensors with red, green, and blue filters.

There are a number of different types of scanners including handheld, flatbed, drum, and film. The handheld scanner is not discussed here as it is slow and fails to produce images that meet the library's digitization requirements.

Flatbed Scanners

A flatbed scanner has a glass pane or platen upon which images to be scanned are placed face down. Beneath the glass is a bright light, which illuminates the pane and an optical array of charge-coupled devices. The charge-coupled devices and light may move beneath the glass or the platen may move across a fixed array of charge-coupled devices. Depending on the quality or density of the scanned image and the speed of operation, the costs for a flatbed scanner can range from $100 to more than $10,000.

Some scanners have document or page feeders to improve the overall throughput rate – 25 to 150 pages per minute.

Drum Scanners

A drum scanner captures image information using a photomultiplier tube (PMT) rather than a charge-coupled device. The original is mounted on an acrylic cylinder (the drum) that rotates at high speed. The drum scanner has three matched PMTs, which read red, blue and green light, respectively. Drum scanners can scan originals up to 11" by 17" (or larger in some cases).

Drum scanners typically allow the operator to separately control sample area and aperture size. The sample size specifies the area that the scanner reads to create each pixel. The aperture controls the amount of light that is being received. The value of the separate control of these two variables is useful for smoothing film grain when scanning film (black-and-white and color) negative originals. Drum scanners can have resolutions up to 12,000 dpi.

Film Scanner

A film scanner is manufactured to scan positive ("slide") or negative film. Typically uncut filmstrips or mounted slides are inserted in a carrier which then moves automatically across a lens and a charge-coupled device scanner.

Digital Camera

Although technically not a scanner, a digital camera can be used to capture an image.

Book Scanner

Two digital cameras are used to simultaneously photograph two adjacent pages in a book for some book scanners. More expensive versions of a book scanner will include a robot that will automatically turn the pages of the book during the scanning process. Some book scanners come with a V-shaped platen to ensure that the spine of the book is not damaged during the scanning process.

Book Scanner

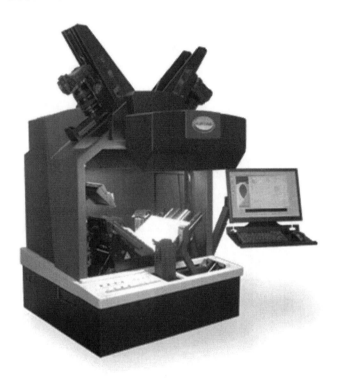

Given the very high costs for purchasing a book scanner, over $75,000 in most cases, a library should have plans to digitize hundreds or thousands of books to make the purchase price cost effective.

An interesting low-cost book scanner from Ion costs $189 and scans 2 pages per second.

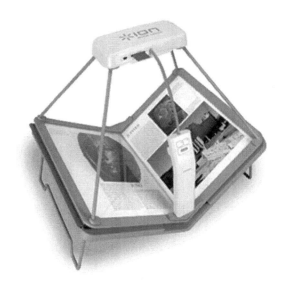

The Ion Book Saver
http://www.ionaudio.com/booksaver

Depending upon the quality of the digital camera, page images can provide an experience that is similar to using the physical book itself. Page images show the exact layout of the page of text and illustrations, capture the full range of colors, show the fonts used for the text, and can show the actual dimensions of the page. Age spots, tears, stains, and notes in the margin can also be shown to the user. The user has the experience of using the book without actually using the book, which is often in frail and fragile condition. The Cuneiform Digital Library (www.cdli.ucla.edu), the Early Manuscripts of Oxford (http://image.oc.ac.uk), and the Nineteenth Century in Print: Books – a part of the American

Memory collection of the Library of Congress (http://memory.loc.gov/ammem/index.html) all provide great examples of viewing page images.

The Computer Connection

Typically a computer workstation is adjacent to and connected to the scanner. Given the large file size of scanned images, the speed with which data is transferred from the scanner is important. The following physical interfaces (identified with increasing data transfer speeds) include:

- General Purpose Interface Bus (GPIB)
- Small Computer System Interface (SCSI)
- Universal Serial Bus (USB)
- FireWire.

Most scanners are bundled with optical character recognition (OCR) software that converts images of text into standard text. The resulting text can then be edited and the text is also used to create an index to the image files.

Periodically the files on the computer workstation are moved to a file server which then can download a copy of a file to a computer located anywhere on the network.

It is vital that procedures be put in place to ensure that a backup of the data is made and that the backup data is moved off-site regularly. With the advent of cloud computing, backups can be scheduled and data moved over the Internet to a remote location without the need for staff involvement.

Optical Character Recognition (OCR)

Optical character recognition works by analyzing a document and converting it into machine-readable digital text. OCR works by breaking up an image into smaller component parts to find text blocks, sentence/line blocks, word blocks and character blocks. The OCR software has a large dictionary of characters from various fonts and languages. When all the characters of a word have been identified, the word is compared to the OCR's dictionary of complete words. The accuracy of conversion is defined as the percentage of correct characters compared to the total number of converted characters.

An accuracy rate of 99.98 percent would be one wrong character out of a total of 5,000 characters. For text created after 1950, an accuracy rate of 99.98 percent is routinely achieved. For materials created between 1900 and 1950, an accuracy rate greater than 95 percent is difficult. Higher OCR accuracy rates are achieved by:

- Using higher-resolution imaging (600 dpi rather than 300 dpi) leads to better OCR accuracy
- Mixed typefaces and complex layouts will typically lead to lower results
- Skewed pages and blurred images result in the "garbage in, garbage out" syndrome
- Smaller typefaces lead to poorer results.

The British Library commissioned a study to examine the OCR accuracy of their 19th Century Newspaper Project.

The results of this analysis (Tanner et al 2009) found:

Character accuracy = 83.6%
Word accuracy = 78%
Significant word accuracy = 68.4%
Words with capital letter start accuracy = 63.4%.

As noted elsewhere in this book, crowdsourcing is one way to improve the quality of the converted text by involving the users of the digital library in improving its digital content.

Born Digital

In addition to converting existing paper-based documents and other objects into digital format, a wide variety of other resources are created in digital form. This digital creation process has been called "born digital." Born digital resources will also need to be carefully maintained and access provided to this material in the coming decades.

Among the many types of born digital materials are:

- *Digital photographs.* The digital library will need to ensure that the photographs are stored in current mainstream formats and are copied onto durable media.
- *Digital documents.* Today almost all documents are created in digital form. Documents must be stored in a standard digital format such as Portable Document Format (PDF).
- *Dynamic data.* This includes data sets that are added to over time or computer-aided design (CAD) files. It may be necessary to maintain both the hardware and software to access this data.

- *Digital art.* While digital art might be digital photographs it may also include mixed media requiring some creative solutions to preserve and provide access to the art.
- *Digital media.* Commercial publications of music CDs, movies on DVD, and video games are all published and as new formats are developed the content is often re-released on the new format. However, as the content loses its commercial value, it may be necessary to preserve this digital material.
- *Harvesting Web content.* An organization may wish to archive its own Web site and the Web sites of other similar organizations to ensure that the content is not lost to future users. The Web harvested data can be kept in WebARChive (an ISO standard) file format (Erway 2010).

Digital Object Identifier (DOI)

The Digital Object Identifier (DOI) is a managed system for persistent identification of content on digital networks and can be used to identify physical, digital or abstract entities. The DOI system was developed and implemented by a number of publishers in the year 2000 and by early 2009 there were over 40 million DOIs. The DOI has been adopted as an international standard. Information about an object can change over time, including where to find it, but its DOI name will not change.

There are four important concepts relating to identifiers: uniqueness, resolution, interoperability, and persistence.

Uniqueness. The identifier (sometimes called a string) should identify one and only one entity. An identifier scheme may allow multiple identifiers for one entity (DOI, ISBN, LCCN).

- *Resolution.* The process in which an identifier is input to a service in order to receive a specific output of information related to the identified entity (the address of the DOI of interest) is called resolution.
- *Interoperability.* The ability to use an identifier for services outside the direct control of the issuing assigner is known as interoperability.
- *Persistence.* Persistence is the necessity that once assigned, an identifier denotes the same item indefinitely (Paskin 2010).

The original DOI participants established a set of 14 metadata elements that support the authentication and protection of intellectual property on the Internet. A subset of these elements forms what is called *kernel metadata* that are the essential elements for interoperability.

Should a library wish to assign a DOI to its digital objects it would need to join the International DOI Foundation (http://www.doi.org/). DOIs should be used if the library is going to license its high-quality images and other electronic resources. Remember that the metadata is subject to the same preservation challenges as the digital resource it supports.

Economics

The costs of the digital library can be conveniently divided into two categories: purchase or up-front costs, and on-going costs.

Up-Front Costs

The up-front costs can be divided into equipment costs, software costs, furniture costs and space modification costs. Depending upon the size of the library and the amount of material to be digitized the budget may be relatively small ($5,000 to $25,000) while for other libraries the initial startup budget may exceed $75,000 if more than one scanner is needed.

On-Going Costs

Once an object is in a digital format, whether a digital representation of a physical object or was born digital, the maintenance costs over time are identical. Among these costs are hardware, software, and personnel.

Hardware costs. Since computer hardware has a finite lifespan, it will need to be replaced on a regular basis. The disk drive on which the digital object is stored will fail and the server(s) will also need to be upgraded. This means that periodically the digital objects will need to be migrated from one piece of hardware to another. The usable lifespan of digital medium varies depending on the choice of medium (Pomerantz and Marchionini 2007). For example, while estimates vary the following illustrates these varying life spans:

- Magnetic tape – 1-2 years

- Magnetic disks – 5-7 years
- Optical discs – 25+ years.

Software costs. The operating system of the server(s) will need to be maintained by installing new releases. In addition, the server operating systems have a life cycle and at some point in time, they will need to be replaced with the latest and greatest. Also, file formats change with new functionality being introduced and new application software being developed that requires installation. As a result, digital objects will need to be "ported" or moved from one file format to another format.

Staff costs. Staff is needed to either oversee the outsourcing of all scanning activity or the actual scanning and creation of the associated metadata. A recent survey (Primary Research Group 2010) found a mean of three (3) staff members devoted to digital efforts (the median was two) among the responding organizations. Make sure that the work between scanning and metadata is balanced although in most cases, staff will spend considerably more time creating the metadata than in the process of scanning and creating the digitized object. Student interns might be interested to work on a project to obtain hands-on, first-hand experience with digitization.

It should be noted that staff could spend between 30 and 40 percent of their time organizing materials for the process of digitization. This includes organizing the materials, assigning unique ID numbers to each item or folder, and ensuring that copyright permissions have been obtained (if the library is not the copyright owner). A sample budget for ongoing digitization within a library assuming two staff members are dedicated to this task is shown in Table 8-1. A library can easily adjust this sample budget by changing the amount of the salary and benefits, cost of the scanner, and so forth.

The amount of material that can be digitized each month will depend on the type of material, the type of scanner being used, and the experience of the staff. At the start of a project, staff should document the time spent on various activities while they digitize a sample of the project materials. Once this is done, the library can then more accurately estimate the time and costs to digitize a specific collection.

For the really small library (one or two professionals) recognize that any digitization project is a time consuming activity and it is important to develop realistic expectations about what can and can't be done while attending to the regular day-to-day activities in the library. It would be smart to start small, explore alternatives for collaboration, and consider outsourcing the digitization of materials to a service bureau.

Grants and the Ongoing Budget

Many libraries have been able to demonstrate need to government agencies and foundations and thus receive grants to support the startup and ongoing costs for a 2-3 year period. The good news is that the library has received the funds and can accomplish some digitization goals. The bad news is that the library is committed as a part of the grant process to deliver some very specific deliverables within a designated time period. Grant monies are not available for the cost of maintaining and preserving things digital and, over time, these costs will only grow larger as additional content is added to the digital library.

Ultimately the library will need to plan for and include in its regular budget all of the costs for the support of a digitization/preservation program as well as support the library's digital library presence in cyberspace. Note that some libraries who have been involved in creating and expanding a digital library for some years find the "invisible nature" of the digital library to be problematic when presenting the associated costs to funding decision makers during the budgetary process.

Many libraries make low resolution images available for use online. If an individual would like to use a high-resolution image for some purpose, many libraries require licensing and the payment of a fee. The revenues thus generated help to operate the digital library while at the same time providing free open access to the content of the digital library.

Many libraries have found that when a digital collection is no longer updated or the Web site is not kept refreshed so that the user experience improves over time, users are quick to abandon the site. Staff need to be available to resolve problems quickly as well as to add content or improve the usability of the Web site by providing additional context.

Staffing Implications

Staff members that assume responsibility for digitization efforts in a library must be trained both in the use of the scanning equipment, creating the necessary metadata and ensuring that standards adopted by the library are being met. This will likely mean that selected staff members will need to travel to receive the necessary training.

Library staff will need a broad range of skills or competencies when working in a digital library. Some of these skills will overlap the skills needed in the traditional library while other skills are new. The library should update job descriptions to incorporate new Web-related tasks and digitization skills. Whenever a job opening occurs due to retirement or transfer, think about the skills the library will need in the future. Don't automatically assume the same set of skills is still needed. Among the skills needed are (adapted from Choi & Rasmussen 2009):

Competency	Content
Knowledge organization	-Metadata creation & other issues -Data organization & retrieval standards & practices
Knowledge dissemination	-Information retrieval & use of resources in multiple formats -Public & service orientation
Knowledge accumulation	-Interest in instructional services -Teaching/training skills -Able to absorb new information quickly -Professional & scholarly activity
Technical skills	-Designing & improving user interfaces -Information architecture -Understanding database technologies -Use of markup languages (XML, HTML)
Resource building	-Digital scanning & imaging/Photoshop skills -Creation, development, and management of digital information/digital document collections -Use of OCR software -Scholarly information trends -Electronic/digital resources
Institutional management	-Communication & interpersonal skills -Project management skills -Planning & organization skills -Management & supervisory skills -Understanding the organizational environment -Writing reports -Understanding intellectual property rights
Personal attributes	-Capacity to work independently -Desire to learn constantly and quickly -Willing to be flexible -Ability to work collaboratively with others -Skill at enabling and fostering change -Propensity to take risks -Desire to work at the leading edge and not the bleeding edge of technology

In addition, since staff members in a digital library will often be working as a team, good communication skills will become even more important – especially when staff members are working from different locations. Thus, staff members will need to be able to work independently, be willing to embrace change and to learn new skills as the technology continues to evolve while being fully responsive to the digital library customers.

A recent survey by the Library of Congress Digital Preservation Outreach and Education initiative found that (Library of Congress 2011):

- Half of the responding organizations (libraries, museums and archives) had less than 25 employees
- One-third of the respondents had some staff dedicated to preservation activities. One-half of the respondents devoted staff as needed.
- Most respondents felt the need for more technical training
- The preferred format for training was the small, in-person workshops of the half-day or full-day variety
- Almost all (95 percent) of digital content holdings consisted of digitized versions of already-held collections.

Space Implications

The library will need to allocate space for the scanner(s), work areas to organize paper files, space for a computer workstation, and other needs that may arise. One rule of thumb suggests a minimum of 350 to 500 square feet per staff member involved with digitization. In addition to scanners, computer workstations, space for paper files and materials to be scanned, space also might be needed for light tables, sorting and organizing tables and other related equipment.

Organizing space for a digitization lab will require some lead-time and planning. While most plans will come together fairly smoothly, it is important to remain flexible and recognize that some problems will inevitably crop up and will need to be dealt with.

Some libraries have created digital labs where the work of digitization takes place. In some cases, these digital labs are very visible and used to market the digital library as a way to encourage individuals to donate scholarly information to the library so that it can be preserved and digitized. Other libraries have placed the digital lab in the "back room" or have not created a lab but rather rely on outsourcing the process of digitization.

Workflow Implications

Prior to starting the digitization process, the library should establish a set of standards that will be followed. These standards should specify the quality of the resulting digital objects, how quality will be periodically tested to ensure adherence to the standards, a file naming scheme established, and a dedicated directory should be created to receive the digital files. The standard should also establish metadata standards for each digital object.

Principles for Digitized Content

1. Digital libraries *are libraries*. The policies of the American Library Association apply fully to digital libraries including such values as commitment to access, confidentiality privacy, the public good, and professionalism.
2. *Intellectual property rights*. Digital content protected by copyright should be protected in a fair and equitable manner.
3. *Sustainability* requires secure and ongoing funding, technology solutions that are appropriate to the longevity of the cultural record, and long-term management capabilities.
4. *Collaboration* enables the building of collections to support research, scholarship and information needs of diverse communities. Collaboration will require strong organizational support and promotion by cultural heritage professionals, their institutions, and their associations.
5. *Advocacy.* The library and cultural heritage community must reach out to the public, to government, and to funding institutions with a clear and compelling message regarding the role of digital libraries and collections.
6. Digital collections address an *international* audience and are part of a global information infrastructure that is not limited by geography.
7. Members of the cultural heritage professions must engage in *continuous learning* and be able to explore new technology, to work with new partners, and to reach new audiences.
8. *Preservation* activities require the development of standards and best practices as well as models for sustainable funding to guarantee long-term commitment to these materials.
9. *Standards* assist the library in maximizing the usefulness of digital collections. Standards must serve the broadest community of users, support sustainable access and use over time, and provide user functionality that promotes the core library values.

Principles for Digitized Content adapted from the American Library Association's Task Force on Digitization Policy.

Available at:

http://www.ala.org/ala/aboutala/offices/oitp/PDFs/Princip lesfinalfinal.pdf

Digital Collection Development Policy

The library should also create a digital collection development policy that will address what factors are used by the library to determine what materials will be digitized and what materials will be ignored. A part of this process should specify how the library would respond to customer requests for the digitization of specific materials. It may be that some materials will be digitized for a particular request but the images not be kept and little or no metadata be created. Initially the library is encouraged to create collection-level descriptions rather than item-level descriptions. The "More Product Less Process" approach codifies what curators and archivists have been doing all along: foregoing item-level descriptions and instead describing at the series or collection level thus making them more accessible to researchers (Greene and Meissner 2005).

Establishing the standards removes the necessity for individual decision making for each item and smooths the workflow process (Gueguen & Hanlon 2009). Some libraries have established a policy where requests for scanning specific content is given the highest priority and the quickest turn-around time.

While the paper feeding and scanning process can be automated to some degree, humans must be heavily involved throughout the entire scanning process. Documents must be carefully inspected and organized to ensure that they are in the right order and are prepared in such a way as to eliminate damage to the original during the scanning process.

Once the image has been created, an operator may need to check that the image meets minimum standards. The OCR conversion process may need to be checked to make sure that the resulting text does not have an error rate that exceeds minimum standards.

A staff member may create some descriptive metadata that is associated with an image or a group of images. Initially the metadata might be relatively brief to act as a placeholder. The metadata can subsequently be enriched and lengthened as needed by other staff members.

If the library is using a harvester (a software program) with other digital libraries to import metadata and/or metadata plus the digital objects then it will need to have and use on a regular basis a link checking software program. Across the Internet, the rate at which once-valid links start pointing to non-existent addresses, often times called *link rot*, can be as high as 20 percent within a 6 month period. That means as many as 1 in 5 of all links will break - thus the need for the link checking software program.

Important questions for the library to consider and resolve include:

- Who will create the metadata – catalogers or technicians? Once created, should the metadata be reviewed and approved by someone?
- Where will the metadata be stored – with images, with other files, in a separate database, in multiple locations?
- With whom will the metadata be shared - exchange partners (other digital libraries), bibliographic utilities (OCLC), search engines?
- How will the metadata be maintained? Links to other files, whether on a server in the local library or found on the Internet, will need to be verified that the link is still valid.

Insource or Outsource?

Some libraries outsource the actual scanning work of some or all of the material to be digitized to an outside vendor. In some cases, for large maps and other large objects, it is best to use an outside vendor rather than purchasing an expensive scanner that would be used infrequently. A Request for Proposal (RFP) for digitization work should obtain the following information that can be used to evaluate the capabilities of each vendor (RLG 1998):

- Provide a physical description of the materials to be digitized and have the vendor provide assurances that they can handle all of the materials.
- Does the vendor offer color, gray scale and/or bitonal scans?

- What is the maximum dpi possible for each scanner?
- Does the vendor provide JPEG, TIFF, and/or GIF files?
- What is the percent accuracy for OCR conversion of characters, words?
- Does the vendor provide PDF and text files?
- Does the vendor provide single page or bound PDF?
- Will the vendor provide metadata and in how much detail?
- How are the digital image files returned to the library (storage medium)?
- What is the cost of the service given the volume of work included in the library's RFP?
- What is the turnaround time for the work?
- What standards are used to determine quality?

Risk

As hardware and software become obsolete, the digital objects and metadata that depend on them become unreadable – held captive to their own encoding. Companies go out of business or they stop supporting older versions of hardware and/or software. The result is the orphaning of proprietary technologies (would your library be able to read data from 3 ½ inch, 5 ¼ inch or 8 inch floppy diskettes?). The vulnerable elements of the technical infrastructure for digital libraries include:

- Storage media, due to physical deterioration, mishandling, improper storage, and obsolescence
- File formats and compression schemes

- Device, software programs, operating systems, access interfaces, application programming interfaces (API), and protocols
- Distributed retrieval and processing tools, such as embedded scripts (Java) and applets
- Gaps in institutional memory due to technical staff turnover (Rieger 2000).

Summary

Deciding to digitize some of the library's collection raises some important issues that must be addressed during the planning process. Aside from providing the staff and space to accomplish the work, the library must adopt a set of standards that specify how the digital images and digital content will be created and preserved.

Technology, due in part to its unique jargon and the nerdiness factor, can be a bit confusing to the uninitiated. However, any library director should know some basic things about technology that will enable them to be a more effective manager. The "top ten things library administrators should know about technology" was created by library technology guru Roy Tennant (2009) who provides great guidance to the beginner.

Top Ten Things

1. Technology isn't as hard as you think it is. Many of the basic technology services are quite easy and fast to accomplish.
2. Technology gets easier all the time. Software developers make the process of software installation and support easier each year.

Top Ten Things - continued

3. Technology gets cheaper all the time. Thanks to the competitive marketplace the same information technology gets cheaper with each passing year.

4. Maximize the effectiveness of your most costly technology investment – your people. Get your staff all the desktop memory and computer processing power they need (it's cheap) so that they are as productive as possible. And invest in their training so they can keep their skills current.

5. Iterate, don't perfect. Software companies learned long ago that it is smart to release software early (knowing it is not perfect) and iterate rapidly by incorporating the comments of users.

6. Be prepared to fail. Try things out to see what works and what doesn't. Not everything will work but you can learn something and move on.

7. Be prepared to succeed. Introducing something new requires full administrative support in order to get the word out and get people to start using the new "thing."

8. Never underestimate the power of a prototype. Prototypes are faster and easier to try out a new idea and are useful in getting people to react to something concrete.

9. A major part of good technology is good project management. Using teams of people with complementary skills will help bring projects in on time and under budget.

10. The single biggest threat to any technology project is political in nature. A library administrator must throw their support behind a project or use of a technology if it is going to succeed in your organization.

Survival Guide Tips

Even more important than food, having access to drinkable water is key to surviving in an emergency situation. If you were to find yourself in a remote environment, perhaps the most important part of your planning is determining the places you will be able to find drinkable water. Water is even more important in warm or hot territories where the human body evaporates a fair amount of moisture.

- Is your library able to clearly answer the six important questions – Why?, What?, Who?, How?, Where?, and When?

- Recognize that the goal of digitization is to safeguard the long-term value of the images and the associated costs for creating and providing access to them.

- Recognize that your library will need to develop scanning standards for various types of materials – text, documents, photographs, audio and video files and so forth.

- It is important to determine whether the library will purchase equipment to accomplish the digitization of objects or rely on a commercial service bureau.

- High-end digital masters can be used to create lower quality digital objects that can be shared. The library may want to license use of the high-end digital masters.

Survival Guide Tips – continued

- **Recognize that creating and maintaining digital resources is an expensive process.**

- **Library staff members will need new skills that will require training on an ongoing basis.**

- **Creating metadata for the digital collection can consume as much as a third or more of the library's budget to create a digital library.**

- **Be flexible and maintain a sense of humor as you move more and more into the digital library future.**

Short Definitions

- Digital – Using numbers to represent information
- Binary – A number system in which each number is expressed in powers of two using only two digits – zero and one
- Bit – Binary digit
- Byte – Eight bits
- Pixel – Picture element, the smallest addressable screen element
- Pixel size – The proportion of the pixel grid that can be detected and coded by a scanner
- Resolution – Number of pixels (in both height and depth) making up an image
- Dynamic range – Number of possible colors or shades of gray that can be included in a particular image
- Tone – The degree to which an image conveys the luminance ranges of the original scene.

Table 8-1. Sample Library Digitization Budget

Item	Cost
Initial Capital Expenditure	
A single scanner	$10,000
High-end computer workstation	$2,500
Scanner related software	$5,000
Server & disk drives	$10,000
Total CapEx	$27,500
Annual Costs	
Equipment replacement/upgrade fund (20% of CapEx)	$5,500
Software replacement/upgrade fund	$2,500
Supplies	$500
Staff: 1 professional (salary + benefits) 1 clerk (salary + benefits)	$60,000 $30,000
Copyright permissions	Unknown
Total Annual Costs	$100,500

Chapter 9

Preservation

P reservation is an umbrella under which most librarians and archivists cluster all of the policies and options for action, including conservation treatments. The role of museums, archives and libraries to assemble and organize documentation of human activity where it can be protected and used has been recognized for a long time. Information has been embedded in a wide variety of formats, which are preserved so that they can be used by future generations for all kinds of purposes.

Microfilm has been the primary approach to preservation for several decades and will remain viable for years to come. Methodologies have been developed to ensure the accurate representation of the original and if the microfilm is kept in a carefully controlled climate its readability is ensured for many decades. Librarians, curators and archivists have developed tools to monitor the quality of the equipment at the time of image capture, quality of film processing, and sampling the resulting microfilm to ensure minimum preservation standards are achieved.

Yet, we are at the beginning of an era in computer technology that allows digitized images to be used cost effectively for preservation and access of many types of visual materials. Advances in computer technology continue at an unrelenting pace and as Moore's Law suggests computer capabilities double every 18-24 months. This portends significant change as libraries and archives move to embrace digital technologies for preservation purposes.

Regarding digital imaging, important questions that must be addressed are:

- Will the medium's reading device (drive) and its controlling software (driver) remain available and operational?
- How long will the digital images last on the medium?
- Does the digital image reflect sufficient quality?
- Does the compression technique (proprietary or standard-based) involve acceptable risks and should compression be used?
- Is the logical formatting of the data documented and will it be clear to future generations?
- Can the data be moved from one generation of hardware to the next without the loss of data?
- What are the short-term and long-term costs associated with digital imaging?

The single most important element in any preservation program is that of stabilizing and protecting collections. Thus, libraries, archives and museums create and maintain a benign environment that is designed to slow the ongoing deterioration of the whole collection. Organizations with materials to preserve will prepare a preservation survey that documents the physical condition of materials in the collection. A preservation survey is typically the first step when planning and implementing a preservation program in a library.

A preservation survey is conducted by collecting data on a random sample of items. Many surveys conducted in large research libraries in the 1980s and 1990s found as much as 90 percent of the volumes contained acidic paper and that many volumes were brittle and disintegrating. Some of the preservation surveys used a very large sample size and the results revealed a real need for preservation action. For example, the Yale University Library found that 13 percent of items needed immediate repair while 37 percent of books were printed on brittle paper (Walker et al 1985).

After an item has been preserved in some manner, microfilmed or digitized, the library must make a decision as to whether the physical item should be set aside and preserved or discarded. Some of the criteria that should be considered in making this decision are:

- Is there artifactual value? Is the item important for its physical characteristics? Does the item have provenance, exhibition value, or aesthetic qualities that recommend preservation?
- Is the item important to better understand a topic or field of research?

- Is the item complete? Are there any missing pages or sections of a page excised?
- Has the item been heavily used or not used in the last ten years?
- Any constraints caused by copyright law?
- Is the item fragile or in danger of being lost?
- Does the item have permanent research value?

Those concerned about preservation of materials have been attracted to microfilm since a relatively inexpensive photographic process produced huge space reductions. In addition, a copy could be used in place of fragile originals. Newspapers, due to their size and fragile and deteriorating state, were typically the first to be microfilmed.

The advantages of microfilm are that the content is of high quality and the film itself is durable and is viewed as a long-term preservation medium. Yet these positive attributes are of interest to the librarian and not the user.

Even a casual observation will reveal that microfilm readers go unused while computer workstations often have people waiting for their use. Some of the disadvantages of microfilm include:

- There is no full-text searching of microfilm. Readers must wade through a flood of frames to discover the content of interest.
- A physical visit to the local library is required to use microfilm resources.
- Microfilm readers are difficult to use (if they work at all).

- Microfilm can only be used by one-person at-a-time while many thousands can simultaneously access a computer resource.

A more detailed discussion about preservation and conservation of material formats is beyond the scope of this book. For more information see the Preservation Resources sidebar.

Preservation Resources

Paul Banks and Roberta Pilette. *Preservation: Issues and Planning.* Chicago: American Library Association, 2000.

Barbara Higginbotham and Judith Wild. *The Preservation Program Blueprint.* Chicago: American Library Association, 2001.

Sherelyn Ogden (Ed.). *Preservation of Library & Archival Materials: A Manual.* Andover, MA: Northeast Document Conservation Center, 1999.

Archives

"We are in the midst of a historic "upload,"
a frenetic rush to transfer the vast wealth
of analog culture to the digital domain.

Mass digitization of print, images, sound
and film/video proceeds apace through
the efforts of actors public and private,
and yet it is still barely understood how
the media of the past ought to be preserved,
presented and interconnected for the future.

How might we bring the records of our culture
with us in ways that respect the originals
but also take advantage of new media
technologies to enhance and reinvent them?"

Ben Vershbow (2007)

Archives are the raw materials of the history of an
organization, a community or a nation. Archives must
be prepared to keep materials for very long periods of
time – certainly longer than the lifecycle of an existing
computer system. Typically archives distinguish
between *conservation* (which focuses on the condition
of an individual item) and *preservation* (which attempts
to retain the content even if the original artifact is
destroyed or is decaying). In the United States, the
National Archives and Records Administration (NARA)

has the responsibility of keeping some records "until the end of the republic."

Archives must pay a great deal of attention to the issues of security, backup, preservation, conservation, and providing long-term access to information.

Items or materials that must be converted into a digital format are often deposited into an archive or in the Special Collections area of a traditional library. Digital archiving raises some new and very challenging issues.

Digital archiving uses techniques such as *refreshing* (attempting to preserve the precise sequence of bits) and *migration* (which preserves content at the semantic level even if the exact sequence of bits is not preserved).

The artifact type or form of the material can have an impact on how the material is captured in digital form. Among the many artifact types are:

- Books
- Forms
- Magazines
- Manuscripts
- Newspapers
- Photographs
- Posters.

The physical features or properties of an item can influence the manner in which it can be scanned. Among these physical features are:

- Bound
- Transparent

- Reflectivity
- Brittleness
- Rate of decay
- Size – larger items may require special equipment for scanning.

The material content consists of the visible information in the physical material. This material content might be typeset or handwritten text, line art, engravings, half tones or continuous tone regions. In addition, the physical artifact itself might have value in and of itself. Clearly the original of the Declaration of Independence has more value than a copy of the document made one hundred years ago, fifty years ago, or made last year.

The *electronic content* represents the primary choices made about the quality of the digital images while the *electronic form* or *file type* serves as a container for the resulting data. Spatial resolution determines the minimum feature size discernible in the digital image.

The type of material and its associated physical features combined with the choices made about the resulting quality of the digital image after the scanning process will determine the specific manner in which the digital image is captured.

However, none of today's digital media has a very long life. Thus, the risks are high to be able to access digital content given the very short life span of digital media. Given the short life span of digital media, every digital library must plan to refresh their collections on a regularly scheduled basis. Most of the challenge in refreshing digital collections is organizational rather than technological.

Yet, in some respects the refreshing of the digital collections is the easiest problem to confront. The digital content is useless unless the formats, protocols and metadata can be recognized and utilized as technology changes and evolves. New file formats will be developed and become either a real or de facto standard within the computer industry. Old file formats will no longer be supported and will fall out of favor. A computer program is needed to read, interpret and present the data to the user. Thus, the computer program and its associated computer equipment must be preserved in running order to assist in the migration of data from one system to another. Eventually it will be necessary to migrate the data and all other elements (formats, metadata, protocols, application programs) from an old system to a new system. Thus, while the formats and structure of the data may change, the semantics of the underlying content is preserved.

The decision about whether the original material object should be retained by the library is dependent upon a number of factors. These are the same factors libraries use to weed (discard) their existing physical collections. For example, some libraries are keeping microfilm copies of materials that are disintegrating as part of their preservation strategy. And yet the library is also digitizing the microfilm in order to improve access to the content.

Repositories

"[The institutional repository] is like a roach motel.

Data goes in, but it doesn't come out."

Dorothea Salo (2008)

Over the last several years, academic libraries have embraced the concept of digital repositories as a way to preserve and provide access to digital campus assets. Despite the enthusiasm of libraries to organize and encourage the use of the repository, faculty has been slow to contribute content. Having the infrastructure in place and the ability to articulate the benefits of a repository will help establish the library as a meaningful partner on campus.

Digital repositories can be divided into two broad groups: an institutional repository and a disciplinary repository.

An institutional repository increases the visibility of an institution's scholarship providing free public access to that scholarship. Other attractive aspects of the intuitional repository include preservation of the institution's scholarly and administrative assets, providing assistance in managing research data, and exploring alternative models for scholarly communication. The institutional repository clearly addresses an issue of gaining access to scholarship that has been restricted by the high costs of journals. In 2008, Harvard University became the first US higher education institution that mandated faculty to place the final form of all articles in the university's open access institutional repository. Some government agencies require that all published research resulting from a grant provided by that agency be placed in an institutional repository and/or in a disciplinary repository.

Disciplinary repositories also have an important place in the scholarly communication process and libraries have been active in the development and operation of such repositories. The preeminent disciplinary repository is *PubMed Central*, the National Institutes of Health's (NIH) public access repository. Effective April 2008, all recipients of NIH funding were mandated to deposit any articles that resulted from their grants into the open access PubMed repository.

Other disciplinary repositories of note include the *Virtual Observatory* (VO) created by librarians in collaboration with astronomers at Johns Hopkins University; *Genbank* for gene sequences; the *Genome-Wide Association Studies* data repository for genotype and phenotype data; and the *Inter-University Consortium for Political and Social Research*. Other disciplinary repositories that may be of interest may be found in the "Disciplinary Repositories" sidebar. A ranking of world repositories can be found at: http://repositories.webometrics.info/toprep.asp

Disciplinary Repositories

Discipline	Repository
Agriculture	AgEcon – ageconsearch.umn.edu Nat. Agriculture Library Digital Repository – ddr.nal.usda.gov Virtual Open Access Agriculture & Aquaculture Repository – voa3r.eu
Archaeology	Open Archaeology Collection – okapi.berkeley.edu/openarchaeology
Arts	Kultur – culture.eprints.org ART-Dok - archiv.ub.uni-heidelberg.de/artdok/?source_opus=&la=en

Discipline	Repository
Biology/Life Sciences	CiteBank – citebank.org Nature Precedings – precedings.nature.com Threatened & Endangered Species Document Repository – dodtes.nbii.dod.gov/portal/server.pt
Classics	Classics Research Network http://www.ssrn.com/crn/index.html
Computer Science	Computing Research Repository http://arxiv.org/corr/home Association for Computing Machinery http://www.acm.org/ Networked Computer Science Technical Reference Library http://www.ncstrl.org/ Association for the Advancement of Artificial Intelligence http://www.aaai.org/home.html
Cultural Studies	Cultural Studies e-Archive http://culturemachine.tees.ac.uk/VLE/DOMAIN/CSEARCH/TABS/Search.asp Eighteenth Century Studies http://18th.eserver.org/
Earth Sciences	Earth Prints http://www.earth-prints.org/ Karst Information Portal http://www.karstportal.org/ Share Geo Open http://www.sharegeo.ac.uk/
Economics	Economists Online http://www.economistsonline.org/home

Discipline	Repository
Education	ALT Open Access Repository http://repository.alt.ac.uk/ Higher Education Empirical Research http://heerd.open.ac.uk/ Open Educational Resources Research http://oer.issuelab.org/research Technology Enhanced Learning http://www.telearn.org/ Multimedia Educational Resource for Learning & Online Teaching http://taste.merlot.org/index.html Shareable Online Learning Resources http://solr.bccampus.ca/wp/
Environmental Science	Centre for Environmental Data Archive http://cedadocs.badc.rl.ac.uk/
Humanities	Humanities ePrints http://www.hprints.org/
Law	Bepress Legal Repository http://law.bepress.com/ Legal Article Research Portal http://litilaw.lexbe.com/
Library & Information Science	LIS Repository http://dlist.sir.arizona.edu/arizona/ Librarians Digital Library https://drtc.isibang.ac.in/handle/1849/1
Marine Science	Aquatic Commons http://aquaticcommons.org/ India's National Institute of Oceanography http://drs.nio.org/drs/index.jsp Marine & Ocean Science ePrints Archive http://sabella.mba.ac.uk/ OceanDocs http://www.oceandocs.org/ Woods Hole Open Access Server https://darchive.mblwhoilibrary.org/

Discipline	Repository
Mathematics	Archive for physics, mathematics, computer science and statistics http://arxiv.org/ The Electronic Library of Mathematics http://www.maths.soton.ac.uk/EMIS/ELibM.html
Medicine	Minority Health Archive http://minority-health.pitt.edu/ India's OpenMED http://openmed.nic.in/ PubMed Central http://www.ncbi.nlm.nih.gov/pmc/
Philosophy	Ethics in Science & Engineering National Clearinghouse http://www.umass.edu/sts/digitallibrary/ Philosophy Research Network http://www.ssrn.com/prn-/index.html Philosophy of Science Archive http://philsci-archive.pitt.edu/
Physics	CERN Document Server http://cdsweb.cern.ch/ Magnetic Resonance Online Texts http://www.ebyte.it/library/refs/MROnlineTexts.html Nanoscience Archive http://www.nanoarchive.org/
Psychology	Psychology ePrints http://htpprints.yorku.ca/ PsyDok (English & German) http://psydok.sulb.uni-saarland.de/
Social Sciences	Digital Repositories E-Science Network http://www.dresnet.net/ Refugee Research Network http://pi.library.yorku.ca/dspace/handle/10315/2590 Social Science Research Network http://www.ssrn.com/

Any repository will experience more use if the trustworthiness of the repository can be improved. This can, in part, be accomplished by indicating the criteria, if any, for accepting content into the repository and by attaching metadata to the digital content indicating whether it has undergone peer review and/or previously been published. Many users will assume that that the reputation of the university applies uniformly to all of the works in the repository. If the repository is enhanced to provide tools to encourage brainstorming, networking and collaborating then a community of like-minded users may slowly emerge. Any repository must be sensitive to the needs of both contributors and the users who come seeking to download documents (St. Jean et al 2011).

Summary

The digitization of library collections, especially the unique materials often found in the library's special collections, afford the world 24/7 access to this digital content while eliminating the need to physically travel to the library to view and use the content. Yet, the process of digitization also raises some associated issues of preservation that must be addressed by the library. The development of clear policies will do much to avoid the use of ad hoc and case-by-case methods in digitizing a library's collections.

Survival Guide Tips

Food is also important in order to keep up the strength of an individual as they struggle to survive in an emergency situation. Most people do not think to carry very much food when they travel so knowing how to live "off the land" is clearly an important skill if survival is the goal.

- Establishing preservation standards for the materials to be digitized is an important step so that decisions made by staff are not made on an ad hoc basis.

- Examining the digital environment from the perspective of preservation will raise a number of issues that must be addressed by the library. For example, how long should a digital image be stored on a magnetic disk drive before it is refreshed?

- A yearly review of existing standards to determine if they are still the appropriate standard or if a new standard is being embraced by the profession that the library should follow.

- Develop a checklist of questions that should be asked about preserving the materials after they have been digitized.

- Does the library have materials that should be archived and preserved?

- Should the library consider establishing and maintaining a repository for its parent organization?

Chapter 10

The Value of a Digital Library

"I conceive that the great part of the miseries of mankind

are brought upon them by false estimates

they have made of the value of things."

Benjamin Franklin

The challenge for any library as it moves more and more into an all-digital environment is how to provide real value in the life of its customers? Since the 'library as place' ceases to exist in the digital world, the digital library must then find ways in which it is valuable to its customers.

Historically libraries have attempted to demonstrate their value by using a variety of measures and approaches. Among these approaches, in increasing order of complexity, are: usage, measures of outcomes, contingent valuation, and return on investment (ROI).

Usage

Clearly even a cursory examination of any number of statistics will demonstrate that library eResources of all kinds – eJournal articles, eBooks, audio and video, images and so forth – are being downloaded with every increasing frequency. The use of the library's eResources by students, faculty, organizational members and the general public *implies* that these resources are of value to them. The challenge, of course, when making any assumption is that the downloaded item was useful (or even read).

A library can collect usage data from library usage logs, vendor reports (specifically COUNTER-compliant reports), and surveys of use. The usage logs and vendor reports are unobtrusive measures of implied value and can be automatically generated. One challenge when relying on vendor reports is that not all vendors provide reports that are Release 3 COUNTER-compliant (Counting Online Usage of NeTworked Electronic Resources). Each library should insist that the vendors that provide electronic resources (eJournals) provide reports that are COUNTER compliant.

Project COUNTER

The goal of Project COUNTER is to provide credible, compatible, consistent publisher/vendor-generated statistics to the library community. This is accomplished by defining all terms, providing specifications for each data element and report, providing a test bed for each vendor to test and refine their reports as well as having their reports audited. As of January 2011, all vendors should have completed certification that they are COUNTER Release 3 compliant.

In the end, a library will know that they are counting and comparing apples to apples for all vendors that provide COUNTER-compliant reports. This is to avoid the confusion and frustration of trying to figure out the meaning of hits, page views, sessions, searches, and downloads for each vendor's report. Without COUNTER-compliant reports – utter chaos.

For more information visit www.projectcounter.org

The Standardized Usage Statistics Harvesting Initiative (SUSHI) is a Web-based services model for requesting data from the vendor. SUSHI works with another system (library developed or provided by a 3rd party vendor – sometimes called a Usage Management system) to automatically retrieve COUNTER compliant statistics and reports.

When a library provides access to a large number of eResources, usage is highly skewed to a few popular titles while at least a few articles are looked at in almost all journals – another example of the 'long tail' (Nicholas et al 2006). And usage has steadily increased over time for almost every library – regardless of type of library. Implicit in the increased number of downloads is the fact that people are willing to "spend" their time downloading and reading to some extent and thus they receive value in the process. However, it is important to recognize that the mere fact that something is downloaded does not demonstrate how it will be used, if it is used at all, or the level of satisfaction for the user.

A number of studies have demonstrated that the electronic availability of eJournals and other related literature, and to a growing extent eBooks, has been the prime factor why there is a decreasing number of personal visits to the research library (RIN 2007).

One study combined usage data with publication and citation data and found that universities with higher download rates have higher publication rates (RIN 2009). And another study found that readings for research purposes were more likely to be from the library's eResources, were rated highly valuable, and influence the research process in many positive ways (Tenopir et al 2009).

Outcomes

It is possible to provide a general overview of the impact or outcomes that the library has in an academic setting, a library in a corporation or governmental agency, or in a public library setting.

There are two primary research methods used to estimate the value of a library. Both methods rely on a large-scale survey of individuals to determine an estimated value. The two methods are:

- Contingent Valuation
- Return on Investment.

Contingent Valuation

Contingent valuation is a method to assess the benefits of non-priced goods and services (for example, libraries or a specific library service). There are two contingent valuation methods – willingness to pay (WTP) and willingness to accept (WTA). Using the willingness to pay method, the survey respondent is asked to state what they would be willing to pay for a new or improved service. The willingness to accept method asks respondents how much compensation for a decline in or elimination of service they would be willing to accept. For example, the respondent is asked how much their property taxes would need to be reduced for them to accept the closing of a library.

Contingent valuation has been used in a number of corporate and public library settings in an effort to estimate the value of the library. In general, when contingent valuation is used, people estimate the economic value of the library at $4 to $6 for every dollar spent by the library.

Return on Investment (ROI)

In simple terms, a return on investment analysis (ROI), often called a cost-benefit analysis, seeks to estimate and compare costs and benefits of an undertaking. It is important to recognize that it is difficult to accurately calculate or estimate the value of the benefits of a service and that those benefits will occur for many years to come. Costs are much easier to determine, assuming an effort has been made to identify and include all relevant recurring and non-recurring costs. Given this reality it is not surprising that a great many cost-benefit analysis reports will show a bias – benefits invariably exceed costs.

A report that discusses the value of the library in terms of ROI will usually make a statement such as "for every dollar supporting the library, the library sees a return on investment of X dollars" (always more than one dollar).

Academic Libraries

Studies have focused on how access to eJournals has changed the way faculty members work (McClanahan et al 2009). Among the many changes are:

- Faculty have become dependent upon electronic access to eJournals to do their work
- eJournals are conveniently available when the faculty want to gain access which has freed up time for more actual research, reading or writing

(no need to walk across campus to visit the library)

- Reading patterns are broadening – faculty members read more articles within and outside their disciplines
- Faculty share more articles with colleagues and students
- Faculty visit the library less frequently and they have become more reliant on electronic access to content
- As the result of online access, faculty feel that they are doing a better job of keeping up with the developments in their fields.

The academic library's impact on research suggests that a library's collections and its services:

- Are valued by faculty and the library's reputation is used to attract and retain faculty members
- Productive researchers spend more time reading materials obtained directly or indirectly from the library
- Researchers who stay current with the literature in a field write better proposals and receive more funding
- Productive researchers who use library resources make more conference presentations, write more articles that appear in peer-reviewed journals, and contribute to other professional activities
- Productive researchers are awarded more prizes and patents.

In an academic library setting, contingent valuation has been used to ask faculty where they would have gone to find information or services if the library was not available to them (Tenopir & King 2007). The cost to obtain information from another source was $50.70 per article (about $42.80 in reader's time and $7.90 to purchase the article). Using alternatives sources of information cost about 9 times the costs of the library providing access to pJournals and eJournals.

Special Libraries

Determining and communicating the value of the special library (libraries located in corporate, government agencies, medical and not-for-profit organizations) is important to ensure that the library is viewed as a positive resource rather than a "sink hole" that sucks up resources. Typically users of the special library are asked to indicate where their use of the library led to improved productivity, cost savings, or increased revenues. A simple ROI is then calculated that compares the gross estimated benefits to the library's overall budget (Oakleaf 2010).

Some of the positive impacts on organizations that result from the use of the library and its services noted in the research literature include:

- Time saved, reduced labor costs
- Shortened production cycle times
- Improved quality
- Increased sales
- Return on shareholder value
- Improved decision making
- Avoiding duplicating research efforts.

Public Libraries

Almost all cost-benefit or ROI studies that have been
completed to date have been in a public library setting.
These studies demonstrate that the citizens of a
community receive value through their borrowing of
library materials in lieu of purchasing the materials
from other sources. The volume of borrowing is
multiplied by an estimated value for each activity (book
borrowing, DVD borrowing, use of a computer and so
forth) to determine an overall value for the public
library (Matthews 2007).
Almost all of the cost-benefit studies done in a public
library setting indicate that the value of benefits ranges
from $4 to $6 for every dollar in the library's budget.
While some find this finding to be significant and
important others merely yawn and ask "Is that all?"

Summary of Outcome Benefits

Examining the possible economic benefits of using a
library from the customer's perspective, it is possible to
consider three categories of benefits:

1. **Direct Use Benefits** – output and outcomes that
   can be measured directly. Some writers call a
   direct benefit a tangible benefit.
2. **Indirect Use Benefits** or economic impact – the
   intangible outputs and outcomes facilitated by
   the programs and services of a library.
3. **Nonuse Benefits**. The benefits of having the
   resource within the community so that others
   may use or not use the library as they so choose.

The total value of the library to the members of a community, in theory, is determined by adding together the use and nonuse benefits. Value can be thought of as the worth of a product or service in terms of organizational, operational, social, and financial benefit to the customer. All library product offerings and services, whether in the physical library or delivered electronically, have a real value and cost in the mind of the customer. In addition to the actual out-of-pocket costs of getting to the library, other cost factors experienced by the customer include the time and effort to make use of a library service. In effect, the individual customer is performing a quick cost-benefit analysis when considering the potential use of the library – "Do the benefits exceed the costs?" or "Is it worth my time?"

As stated before, in the digital library environment it is crucial to know explicitly how a library adds value in the life of its customers.

Value in the Digital Library

The challenge facing every library today is how to add value in the life of its customers as the library migrates from being a hybrid to a digital library. Historically, libraries provided access to a wide variety of information resources (the library's collections) that had been organized as well as a set of services designed to improve access to the library's collections.

As shown in Table 10-1, libraries are transitioning from the traditional library to the digital library as evidenced from a number of perspectives.

218

Table 10-1. Characteristics of the Traditional and Digital Library

Traditional Library	Digital Library
Library-focused	Customer-focused
Collection-focused	People-focused
Linear	Linked
Expert	Trainer/Learner
Primarily text	Graphic/Multimedia
Static	Interactive & Mobile
Individual	Collective/Community
Owned	Licensed
Query-based	Interactive
Structured	Fluid
Intermediated	Disintermediated
General	Customized
Access	Collaborative production

Now, however, the library must do more than provide access to digital resources – eJournals and eBooks – or otherwise the library's buying and preservation functions can be incorporated into larger organizational settings on a more cost effective basis (cooperatives, regional libraries, state libraries).

A visit to most digital libraries will reveal the presence of a number of collections that have been digitized that can now be accessed. Rather than browsing or searching these digital collections one by one or across all the digital collections simultaneously, the library must do more to provide value for the user of the digital library. So how then does a digital library provide value to its customers?

One important caveat for each digital library is to help the user understand the capabilities and limitations of the system and its associated digital content. Unless the user's expectations are clearly and carefully managed, a number of problems will likely arise. It is important to help the user understand:

- What content will not be found in the digital library
- That a limited amount of primary materials are available online
- That persistence in searching and learning a new user interface will be required
- While there are a number of access points, all of the access points (or indexes) will not be available in each digital collection (Marchionini et al 2003).

In addition to managing user expectations by clearly disclosing what is and is not available within the digital library and its collections, the library can add value by providing content. Context is provided when the user is presented with several ways of navigating the digital content. In addition to searching and serially browsing the digital content, the library might present a timeline to show when in time the digital content was created.

Showing how the digital content is related to geographical places, such as with map collections, can provide additional context. It is possible to link place names or names of people in literary works to specific places on a map. The result then is a digital corpus that is more than the sum of its parts and that evolves over time. Individuals using the digital corpus can make additions, annotations, and corrections (much as they do now in the social networking arena), which will further enhance the value of the digital library.

> "Can you imagine there was a time when the books in a library didn't talk to one another."
>
> Marvin Minsky
> Quoted in Kurzwell (1990)

The idea is to go beyond listing of available digital collections, which are of limited interest and use, to demonstrate how collections relate to one another and can be used to increase knowledge and understanding.

Practical Realities

Despite the fact that libraries have been online longer than most people think, libraries still are the antithesis of the online world. And most people have no idea what a "database" can do for them when they encounter the word on a library Web page. Many people think of something techie and complicated such as relational database product Oracle (or one of its competitors). The notion that someone might find value in a database provided by a library is an utterly foreign concept to many people. Your library needs to find terms that are more user-friendly and descriptive to describe the eResources available to the library's customers.

eResources need to be marketed by topic and communicate how the customer can learn how a particular database or eJournal can assist the customer in solving an information need. Vendors (and libraries) are naive in thinking that a library customer will know what "EBSCOhost," "ERIC," "Factiva," WilsonSelect" can do for them. Grouping databases and eResources by topic will have much more appeal to the library user.

Make sure that the library's Web page has all library jargon removed. John Kupersmith has a Web site that is dedicated to providing more user-friendly terminology that will appeal to almost everyone (visit www.jkup.net/terms). Use of these terms suggested by John will do much to improve the usability of a library Web site.

Make eResources easy to find. Aside from having a prominent location on the library Web site for the "electronic library" (no scrolling allowed), make sure there are multiple links to the eResources from other pages on the library's Web site.

A digital library may need to restrict access to some eResources in order to comply with vendor licensing agreements. In addition, the library may wish to provide access to low resolution images and sell (with restrictions) higher resolution images of the library's digital materials.

The whole notion of a digital library radically changes what it means to "collect." When an electronic collection of eBooks, eJournals, and other electronic resources are always accessible from a desktop computer or mobile device, where the "electronic resource" is actually located becomes meaningless. After all, it is only a copy of the electronic resource that is being downloaded. The challenge for the library is to what extent electronic resources located elsewhere have their associated (harvested) metadata in the library's online catalog?

Libraries also face a dilemma when considering the digitization of their collections, especially their special collections. How much of a library's proven population special collections, e.g., photographs, historical documents, maps and so forth, should the library digitize and make accessible to all? Should the library digitize a complete collection or the full contents of a book or only make selections available? Should the library focus on "important" materials (however important is defined?) or simply the most popular high-demand materials? Clearly any library will need to balance its available resources and create priorities in the creation of its digital library collections.

Most importantly, once a library has digitized one or more collections, it can maximize the visibility and accessibility of these collections using three methods: search engine optimization, the use of RSS feeds, and incorporating content from digital collections into discovery interfaces (Breeding 2009). Search engine optimization ensures that the contents of the digital collections are made accessible to the software robots used by Google and other search engines so that the library's resources are found when someone conducts a search. A RSS feed is an opt-in service that automatically provides information about new resources and provides a link back to the digital library. A new generation of user-friendly online catalog interfaces provides a means to view digital content in a variety of ways that are selected by the user.

A Good Digital Library

Assessing the quality of collections and services provided by any library, digital or otherwise, requires the use of some evaluation criteria. It is possible to utilize evaluation criteria from a number of perspectives as shown in Table 10-2. The library should consider developing a plan for the periodic evaluation of its digital library using a subset of the possible evaluation factors.

Table 10-2. Types of Evaluation Criteria*

Perspective	Type of Criteria

Costs	Total costs
	    Staff costs
	    Information technology costs
	    Electronic resources costs
	    Other costs
	Cost per use

Usability	General usability assessment
	Interface usability
	    Search and browse
	    Navigation
	    Help features
	    View and output
	    Accessibility
	    Terminology
	    Learnability
	    Facilitate interaction between
	        other users & library staff
	Other

Collection Quality	Quality in terms of:
	    Breadth & scope
	    Authority
	    Accuracy
	    Completeness
	    Currency
	    Usefulness
	Other

224

Table 10-2 – continued.

Perspective	Type of Criteria
Service Quality	Mission Market penetration Use of online tools Other
System Performance	Information retrieval Relevance Precision and recall Link maintenance - number of broken links Response times Reliability Interoperability Other
Customer Opinions	User satisfaction User feedback Impact on the user Productivity Other
Use of Library	Number of unique visitors Number of items downloaded Number of links used Number of research/reference questions answered Other
Usefulness	Effectiveness – useful information and resources were located

*Adapted from Xie 2006; Buchanan and Salako 2009

Just as the traditional library is more than the acquisition and maintenance of books, journals and other materials, a good digital library is more than the creation and maintenance of digital objects. The characteristics of a good digital library include:

- Has a digital collection created according to an explicit written collection development policy
- Describes its collections so a user can discover important characteristics of its collections
- Is sustainable over time and does not rely on grant funding for its continued existence
- Is broadly available and uses an easy to learn and easy to use user interface
- Respect intellectual property rights and has received permissions from all necessary rights holders
- Provides links to other digital library collections and ensures that the user is able to understand a broader context for the materials found in the digital library
- Systematically collects measurement of use (Adapted from Cole 2002).

A good digital library will actively recruit the participation of its users to make the digital content better and richer. The digital library should support tagging and allow its users to make corrections to digital content, especially correcting OCR errors. Consider that the National Library of Australia allowed users to tag and correct errors in its Australian Newspapers digital collection. In fifteen months, a little more than 6,000 users corrected 7 million lines of text in 318,169 articles (out of a total of 8.4 million articles). In addition, the users added 197,597 tags (Holley 2010A, 2010B). Interestingly, the users created and enforced their own tagging rules (the library refused to establish any rules). Allowing users to be actively involved in shared digital content is a form of crowdsourcing. Crowdsourcing assists the library in achieving goals that it would not have the time, financial or staff resources to achieve on its own.

Summary

The decisions a library makes about what materials to digitize and make accessible will have a profound impact of the value of the digital library. These decisions also entail how the collections are described and the transparency of the metadata will determine, in part, the degrees to which the digital library resources are discovered in Web search engines. It is difficult to envision a definition of value that does not include use so the degree to which the resources of a digital library are in fact used will play an important part in determining value.

"Librarians and archivists often fall into the error of assuming that academic researchers, if they are information literate, should know about them (the digital library) or how to find out about them or how to use their collections. The simple fact is that most academic scholars are not trained nor experienced in the use of original sources, be it in manuscript of print, much less in the use of non-traditional material such as photographs, prints or God help them, material culture. To catalog is not enough, nor is encoding a finding aid or having the capability of transmitting full text to his or her office PC." (Michel 2005).

For many librarians, the original intent of the digital library was that it would serve as a teaser to the rich special collections of the library. Researchers and scholars would then become aware of the resources and schedule a trip to delve deeper in the collections over an extended period of time. However, almost everyone, including preeminent researchers, want to access to full content of the special collections from their desktop (or mobile device). Remember, convenience trumps everything. And as the costs of scanning and storage of digital objects continue to decline, the possibility of providing access to the complete contents of special collections becomes feasible for even the smallest of libraries. The digital library of the future will provide a bridge to a wealth of digital objects from the everyday person who is interested in a particular topic to an experienced academic scholar.

Survival Guide Tips

After assessing the survival situation that you find yourself in, and having used the map and compass to orient yourself to the locale, it is imperative to plan a course of action for rescuing yourself. In some cases, it might be best to build a shelter and wait for rescue and in other cases it might be best to select a destination that would improve your chances of rescue and survival. Thus, it is imperative to set a goal and act upon it.

- Recognize that the value of a library is primarily based in the use of the library and its resources and services.

Survival Guide Tips – continued

- For a special library, the principal value is based on direct use benefits – does the library save the time of the user? Does the library have resources that assist an individual in saving money for the organization? Does providing access to digital resources improve the productivity of the user?

- For the academic library, the primary value is a combination of direct use and indirect use benefits. Does the library save the time of the user by providing access to resources of value? Do the accomplishments of the user have an indirect benefit for the college or university? Does the student do better academically as the result of using library resources and services?

- Given that resources and services are increasingly provided virtually, the library should be moving in the direction of a more digital library.

- Has the library identified ways in which it can engage its users so that they are direct participants in using and improving library resources through the use of social media or crowdsourcing opportunities? Is the library building a community around its digital library?

- Does the library recognize that the portion of its budget devoted to the creation and maintenance of digital resources will only grow over time?

Chapter 11

Digital Library Best Practices

"Design, in its broadest sense, is the enabler of the digital era. It's a process that creates order out of chaos, that renders technology usable. Design means being good, not just looking good."

Clement Mok

A significant amount of information about digital libraries has been presented in the prior chapters of this book. Clearly there are a number of issues related to creating and maintaining a digital library that must be addressed. Aside from the important issue of communicating the value of the library so that the funding decision makers provide the necessary funds, there are a variety of other important issues pertaining to staffing, intellectual property rights, creating and maintaining digital collections, providing access to the library's digital materials and so forth. These issues have been discussed at some length in the prior chapters of this book.

Some important questions that should be addressed prior to creating a digital library are:

- What is the purpose of the digital library?
- Who will be using the library?
- What are the characteristics and needs of various types of users?

- How will users tend to approach the digital library and its collections?
- What kinds of activities will the users wish to perform?
- Is more than one user interface needed (basic and a more sophisticated interface for the advance user)?
- Will users prefer to explore items within a single collection or will they wish to bring multiple digital objects from various sources together?
- Will the library harvest metadata and/or digital objects from other organizations?

The reality is that the digital library is the intersection of many different disciplines and functional areas and that the opportunities for collaboration are enormous as shown in Figure 11-1. It is important that your digital library reach out in order that it can "become all it can be!"

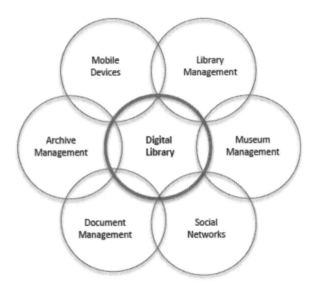

Many decades ago, Shiyali Ranganathan (1931) developed his "Five Laws of Library Science which are presented here in modified form to better reflect the realities of the digital library. With apologies to Ranganathan the "Five Laws of the Digital Library" are:

1. Digital objects are for use.
2. Digital objects for all; every user his digital object.
3. Every digital object its user.
4. Save the time of the user.
5. A digital library is a growing organism.

Given all of the trends happening in the world outside a library, what are the implications for any library? Consider the following realities:

- *The future is digital and libraries must prepare for it.* The ever-increasing amount of "born digital" content means that the value of analog materials will diminish over time.
- *Digitizing unique materials in a library's collection will improve access to that material (provided the digital content is discoverable by Internet search engines).* Remember that discovery occurs outside the library!
- *Libraries must recognize that they will provide access to both analog and digital materials for the foreseeable future – in essence a bifurcated future.*
- *Add value to digital content by encouraging crowdsourcing.* Encourage users to add tags, reviews, comments, make corrections to OCR created text, provide tools for discussion and collaboration. In short, work hard to nurture the growth of a community around the digital library.

- *A library's budget is increasingly being constrained as licensing (renting) access to eResources (rather than ownership) assumes a more prominent position in the budget.* Also, the costs for licensing eResources increase each year.
- *Cooperative efforts with other libraries and other organizations will become an important strategy for a library.* Minimizing the duplication of materials in a library's collection will allow the library to use its remaining resources more wisely.
- *Digital resources – particularly cloud-based services – require new, standards-based tools and services for description, access, use and preservation.* Libraries should cooperatively participate in and demand the development of such standards (Adapted from Hazen 2010).

Best Practices

Surviving and thriving in any new environment is depending upon having the necessary skills and equipment. Just as you would need a map, compass, water bottle, food and other equipment to cope if you unexpectedly find yourself in the Alaska outback, so too you need to have the requisite skills and equipment as you move into the new digital library environment. Initially, every library needs to consider the reality of acquiring the necessary resources to create and maintain a digital library as shown in Table 11-1. It should be recognized that your library might not need to acquire each of the listed resources (in some cases, it may be necessary to have access to the resource for short periods of time). In such situations, the use of consultants or of a scanning service bureau should be considered.

Table 11-1. Checklist of Digitization Resources*

Category	Resources
Personnel	Manager(s) Intellectual property rights specialist Digitizers Catalogers/Metadata Information technology technical support Software programmers Legal advisors Project advisors
Software	Operating systems - Servers - Desktop Applications - Image capture/manipulation - Metadata authoring - Database - Indexing & search engine - Web server Servers Network clients
Storage Devices	Local hard drives Network storage servers

234

Table 11-1 – continued.

Category	Resources
Storage Devices- cont.	Optical devices, e.g., CD/DVD writers Controlled storage environment Off-site backup storage "Cloud-based" disk storage
Network Infrastructure	Routers Switches Network cards Ports Cables
Supplies	Stationery Utilities Printer cartridges Lamps (for image capture devices/special lighting) Storage & backup media
Project Management	Staff recruitment Proposal preparation/evaluation Establishing digitization standards Design of workflow Quality assurance Staff supervision Creation/modification of Web site Publicity/marketing

*Adapted from NINCH 2003.

The digital library and the digitization of printed and analog materials can significantly improve the value of the original collections by opening new doors of understanding for scholars and improving access to individuals around the world. For example, a digital library can:

- Improve the readability of the original by revealing content hidden by deterioration, dirt, stains and aging.
- Provide good quality digital surrogates of art works, maps, posters, photographs, newspapers and other materials that are dispersed in different institutions around the world.
- Improve the ability to search and manipulate text in electronic format offering new ways to discover content. Rather than searching descriptive surrogates (bibliographic records) a user today can search the full text of millions and millions of journal articles, newspapers and books.
- Offer access to different editions and versions of a work. In fact, today many people are combining snippets of text, audio and video content to create new and interesting works.
- Create new indexes, which allow searching of video, audio, or images in new and interesting ways.
- Bring their digital collections to new audiences and facilitate new ways for people to explore and understand the content.

Management Oversight Is Critical

- Develop a digitization strategic plan that identifies criteria that will be used to assess what materials will be digitized
- Establish digitization standards – image quality, converting images to text (establish a maximum error rate)
- Approve specific digitization projects recognizing the resources that will be required to complete a project
- Coordinate the digitization efforts
- Negotiate with groups outside the library
- Promote the library's digitized collections
- Assess user needs – audiences, specific needs, how gain access

Select Collections Wisely

In most cases, only a small proportion of the digital objects will be used over a given time period. One challenge is how to ensure that these less-used materials, which may have significant scholarly value, are preserved? Among the issues that should be addressed are:

- Is there a physical counterpart (print, microform) to the digital object or collection?
- Can the collection be digitized again (perhaps at an higher standard)? What are the associated costs?
- Does the collection fall within one of your institution's subject strengths?
- Do other institutions hold similar digital copies? What is the added value of this local collection?

- Does the digital collection generate income? Is the income sufficient that the digital library is self-sustaining?
- How much use of the collection is occurring? How good are the images and metadata? Should additional sites potentially be involved so that more discovery takes place which leads to more use? Has the Web site been optimized so that search engines rank it high?
- What are the consequences of losing this collection?
- Are their legal or other obligations to maintain the digital collection?
- Keep the library's mission in focus. Develop specific criteria for determining what will be added to the library's digital collections
- Start with a collection of high user interest or high research value
- Some important questions to ask before digitizing a collection include:
  o Is the information content of the printed or analog material high?
  o What is the importance, authority, timeliness and uniqueness of the material?
  o Is the object the original?
  o Is the material complete or are parts missing?
  o Is it up-to-date?
  o Is it accurate?
  o What is the size and dimensions?
  o What is the media type and format?
- Some types of materials warrant extra caution
  o Contemporary literary papers
  o Collections with sensitive information – for example, social security numbers

- o Materials with commercial economic value
- o Materials not intended to be made public (for some period of time)
- Physical condition of the materials. Will some of the materials need to be treated with a preservation process to ensure the integrity of the original before digitization can occur?
- If research value is high and risk is also high, consider making sensitive materials only accessible on-site for a period of time

Proactively Work with Donors

- Ask donors to state any privacy concerns and identify any sensitive materials in the collection
- Identify possible intellectual property issues and get relevant contact information
- Suggest donors transfer copyright to the institution or license their works under a Creative Commons License
- Include statements in your collecting policy and in your deeds of gift or transfer document that:
  - o Ensures that no restrictions are placed on content already in the public domain
  - o Grant license to digitize materials for unrestricted access
  - o Guard against limitations or restrictions on fair use rights (adapted from OCLC 2010).

Ensure Intellectual Property Rights Are Preserved

- Check all files for permissions, rights or restrictions

- Assess rights and privacy issues at the most appropriate level – most often the collection level
- Assess the risks and advantages of relying on the fair use doctrine (in the US) to support public access
- Contact and obtain necessary permissions from the rights holder
- Clearly identify the rights status in the description of the collection – public domain, the institution holds the rights, permission obtained from the rights holder
- Will the library license high-quality copies of the collection?
- Manage copyright permissions
- Document your findings and processes used.

Access Responsibilities

The library should inform the user of:

- Their rights to view and use the digital materials
- All applicable copyrights
- Restrictions on use
- How to obtain permission when use is restricted
- How to cite the resources available to users.

Provide Take-Down Policy Statements and Disclaimers

- Adopt a liberal take-down policy that will remove a digital object for which a copyright issue has been raised. Consider: "This digital collection is accessible for research and education. We have indicated all that we know of the copyright and rights of privacy, publicity, or trademark. Upon request, the library will remove materials from public view while any rights issue is resolved and clarified."

- Use an appropriate disclaimer at the institutional level. Consider: "[This institution] makes digital versions of collections accessible in the following situations:
  o They are in the public domain
  o The rights are owned by [institution]
  o [Institution] has permission to make them accessible
  o The materials are made accessible for research and education purposes as a legal fair use
  o There are no known restrictions on use.

Develop Very Specific Procedures for Scanning

- Develop specific standards for scanning and archiving the high-quality digital object of the original material
- What quality standards will be followed when delivering a digital surrogate (sometimes called the "access surrogate")
- Determine what file format will be used for each type of material
- Calculate a rough estimate of the resulting file sizes and verify that sufficient disk storage space is available
- Agree on a file naming protocol
- Adopt specific quality standards for audio and video content
- Will images of text be converted to computer readable text using OCR?

- What materials will be digitized in-house and what will be sent out to a service bureau (e.g., large maps)?
- Develop a workflow so that the handling of materials is minimized.

The Colorado State University Library developed very specific procedures to be followed for scanning, depending upon the type of material (Zhou 2010). These procedures included:

- Use gray scale images that contain gray scale graphs, such as black-and-white photos; color images for pages that contain color photos or charts, and bitmap images for text-only or text and line art pages.
- When a page contains high definition color or gray scale images, scan in a higher resolution and scan other pages at 400 dpi.
- When the OCR conversion of a page is problematical or the type font is small, scan it at a higher resolution and scan the other pages at 400 dpi.
- When a page contains text and gray scale or color, scan it twice. Modify the resulting images using Adobe Photoshop to combine the best of both scans into one page.

Ensure that Staff Have Equipment & Software So They Are Productive

- Sufficient computer memory (RAM) for speedy retrieval (some of the file sizes will be quite large). Given the very low cost of RAM, there is

no reason not to have the maximum amount of memory
- A large (21 inch or 27 inch) flat screen monitor capable of displaying 24-bit color.

Create the Appropriate Amount of Metadata

- Selecting & developing metadata structure – schema to be used (required or optional), field selection, field labeling, and data dictionary creation
- Selecting and creating controlled vocabularies
- Assigning metadata
- Converting and batch loading of metadata
- Ensuring the quality control of metadata.

Monitor the Quality Control of Digital Content

- Sample the results of digitization to ensure that standards are being met
- Ensure the same people monitor quality and that they receive appropriate levels of training
- Consistently use the same processes to ensure quality
- Use checklists to document quality assurance procedures
- Use resolution and color targets to ensure that the data being captured is consistent and adheres to standards established by the library
- Issues to be checked when checking image quality include:
  - o Image not the correct size
  - o Wrong resolution is used
  - o Wrong file format was selected
  - o Loss of detail in shadows

- o Poor contrast
- o Missing scan lines or pixels
- o Uneven tones or flares
- o Wrong orientation
- o Off center or skewed
- o Incomplete or chopped image
- o Lack of sharpness
- Make sure all outsourced work is reviewed for adherence to quality standards

Provide a User Interface that is Suitable for Digital Objects

- Text image size and quality is important. The completeness and legibility of pages with minimal scrolling is critical. Typically images presented at 200 dpi (originally scanned at 400 dpi) will accommodate differing page and font sizes when presented on a screen of 800 x 600 pixels.
- Graphical image size and quality. Users want the ability to select multiple views of an image to support their different interests and research needs:
  - o Thumbnails should be from 50 to 100 pixels high
  - o Screen size images should average about 400 pixels high
  - o Full-size images should be available (even if they need to be licensed for use)
- Large format graphical images are difficult to display online. Thus, the digital library Web sites should provide tools so that users can zoom, pan and have peripheral-view capabilities.
- Users prefer a simple user interface in order to get to pages that interest them quickly without

the need to page through multi-level menus.
Good design principles include:
- o Flatten the navigation hierarchy
- o Minimize scrolling and jumping
- o Simplify the screen by removing extra text and images
- o Strive for efficiency of the user's task and avoid inconsistencies
- o Choose words carefully and avoid library jargon
- o Support quick judgment of relevance with overviews and descriptions of collections
- o Allow users to add reviews and interact with other users
- Users want to be able to easily navigate the content of image collections. They want to move backward and forward, jump to a specific page or image, view a table of contents or browse an index.
- Users want to manipulate graphical images. Users need to be able to:
  - o Zoom in to see more detail
  - o Examine two or more images side by side
  - o Save and sort search results
  - o Save marked digital objects
  - o Export images into other software
  - o Use image-editing tools
  - o Annotate images with comments and have these remarks saved for other users
  - o Support high-quality printing.
- Periodically test usability of Web interface and revise (to improve).

Preservation of Digital Content is Vital

- Preserve, maintain and refresh digital content

- All archival versions (highest resolution, lossless compression) are written to approved storage media (DVD, disk drives)
- Implement a rigorous off-site backup of digital content

Involve Users and Provide Prompt Feedback

Users may request that the library add, revise or remove digital content. Thus, the library should develop a set of policies to respond to such requests. Requests might raise such issues as:

- Correcting a transcription error
- Correcting a factual error
- Provide a more recent reference (with updated information)
- Misleading descriptions reported in image captions
- Offer to provide digitized materials
- Offer to provide original materials and photographs
- Removal of content for copyright violation
- Request removal of images
- Removal of material potentially libelous (Dawson 2006).

Framework of Guidance

A NISO committee developed a Framework of Guidance that provides guidance around four core types of entities (NISO 2007):

- Collections
- Objects – digital materials

- Metadata – information about objects and collections
- Initiatives – programs or projects to create and manage collections.

Collections

Principle 1: A good digital collection is created according to an explicit collection development policy.

Principle 2: Collections should be described so that the user can discover characteristics of the collection.

Principle 3: A good collection is curated, which is to say, its resources are actively managed during their entire lifecycle.

Principle 4: A good collection is broadly available and avoids unnecessary impediments to use.

Principle 5: A good collection respects intellectual property rights.

Principle 6: A good collection has mechanisms to supply usage data and other data that allows standardized measures of usefulness to be recorded.

Principle 7: A good collection is interoperable.

Principle 8:   A good collection integrates into the
                users own workflow.

Principle 9:   A good collection is sustainable over
                time.

Objects

Principle 1:   A good object exists in a format that
                supports its intended current and future
                use.

Principle 2:   A good object is preservable.

Principle 3:   A good object is meaningful and useful
                outside of its local context.

Principle 4:   A good object will be named with a
                persistent, globally unique identifier that
                can be resolved to the current address of
                the object.

Principle 5:   A good object can be authenticated.

Principle 6:   A good object has associated metadata.

Metadata

Principle 1:   Good metadata conforms to community
                standards in a way that is appropriate to
                the materials in the collection, users of
                the collection, and current and potential
                future uses of the collection.

Principle 2: Good metadata supports interoperability.

Principle 3: Good metadata uses authority control and content standards to describe objects and colocate related objects.

Principle 4: Good metadata includes clear statement of the conditions and terms of use for the digital object.

Principle 5: Good metadata supports the long-term curation and preservation of objects in collections.

Principle 6: Good metadata records are objects themselves and therefore should have the qualities of good objects, including authority, authenticity, archivability, persistence, and unique identification.

Initiatives

Principle 1: A good collection-building initiative has a substantial design and planning component.

Principle 2: A good digital initiative has an appropriate level of staffing with necessary expertise to achieve its objectives.

Principle 3:   A good digital initiative follows best practice for project management.

Principle 4:   A good initiative has an evaluation plan.

Principle 5:   A good digital initiative has a marketing strategy and broadly disseminates information about its progress and outcomes.

Principle 6:   A good digital initiative considers the entire lifecycle of the digital collection and associated services developed.

EOS.Web® Digital

Providing the Ultimate Tools for Digital and Electronic Libraries

Providing your online patrons and staff with remote access to digital, electronic content has just become easier, thanks to EOS.Web Digital. Let EOS.Web Digital streamline your online research, making each search more effective and each minute spent more productive. As a successful digital library, you understand that your electronic information resources are accessed by authorized remote users, staff and research professionals alike. With thousands of libraries already using EOS.Web, you can be certain that we will provide you with the best library automation solution for your digital library. EOS.Web Digital is guaranteed to exceed your library digital automation solution expectations and provide you with the best value in the industry.

All the Tools You Need

Combining a core of powerful EOS.Web tools, EOS.Web Digital provides you with a scalable solution for managing your digital and electronic content. EOS.Web Digital includes all EOS.Web foundation and advanced features, including Electronic Resource Management (ERM) and Electronic Content Management (ECM). With our comprehensive feature set and services, you can be certain that EOS.Web Digital is ideal for your digital library.

EOS.Web Digital Includes:

Electronic Resource Management (ERM) - Effectively manages all electronic resources and Web Subscriptions, such as electronic journals, databases, and electronic books; Completely streamlines the entire electronic resource management process, from a review cycle for the resource record, to purchasing, publishing, and renewing a resource

EOS.Web Digital - continued

Electronic Content Management (ECM) - Routes and maintains electronic serials; Streamlines serial receipt and retention; Allows you to receive, catalogue, and circulate electronic serials easily and efficiently; Automatically archives the issues and then routes a copy via email to a patron list created for particular journals

Content Aggregator - Creates a single location for congregating all of your RSS feeds. The Content Aggregator automatically checks for new content at library-determined intervals and emails the collected information to patrons in a single email, eliminating the disorder caused by separate emails from individual RSS feed sources

Web OPAC - Provides patrons and staff remote access to your electronic collection with any web browser

Cataloging - Full text searching; Individual copy management; Import records from Library of Congress with a single click.

Circulation - Is an intermediary feature for hybrid libraries that are transitioning to full electronic digitization. 'First-available' reservation processing and notification; On-the-fly management options from the circulation station; Self-registration and self check-out functions available through the Web OPAC and Self Check workstation; Automatic email notices to borrowers

Serials Management - Automated electronic check-in processing; Flexible issue prediction system supports varied types of e-journal publication schedules; Claim management automatically identifies electronic subscriptions problems; Record table of contents information or add brief article records

Acquisitions - Allocate encumbered and expended amounts into multiple accounts; Reporting using timeframes, funds, allocations, and more; Allows partial arrival, partial payments, and cancellations; Includes tasks for online periodicals and e-journals, audio, video, and other media types

EOS.Web Digital - continued

Z39.50 Client & Server - International standard protocol for information retrieval between computers; Enables searching and retrieving information from other libraries; conforms to the Bath Profile; allows your catalog to be searched by other libraries using the Z39.50 protocol

KnowledgeBuilder - Classifies "unstructured" information that is not typical of a bibliographic record; Makes items available for on-the-fly, natural language searching customized databases of inhouse defined taxonomies for your unstructured information, even if the files are not stored in the EOS relational database

Reference Tracking - Track and coordinate research requests received by phone, letters, email messages, and faxes; Assures service continuity of research requests by providing a flexible, automated reference query recording system

Indexer - Provides greater access to source materials that need to be indexed and searched, enabling you to build long-term, sustainable custom collections that are cross-searchable; Search custom document collections selected from over 250 different file types in order to acquire knowledge necessary to make mission-critical decisions

IP Authentication - Recognizes and controls user-access of your library's OPAC; Easily and quickly identifies the user's unique identity and location on the Internet; You decide which IP addresses are authorized to access your Web OPAC; Safely access your OPAC from any authorized IP address

Classification Management - Secures information and documentation using security level definitions in the EOS.Web OPAC; Allows library staff to set access levels to sensitive library information items; Security levels are customizable for each client's library

ReportWriter - Allows you to create, edit and manage your own unique reports; Run your unique reports or ad hoc requests for information anytime from anywhere.

Glossary

Aboutness. As used in library and information science, aboutness is considered synonymous with subject.

Access copy. Copy of a digital file that is made available to the user. Typically this copy is of a lower resolution or smaller file size than the master copy.

ACM Digital Library. A digital library consisting of the journals and conference proceedings published by the Association for Computing Machinery.

Administrative Metadata. Data for managing the digital object and providing more information about its creation and constraints governing its use.

Alexandria Project. A geospatial digital library based at the University of California, Santa Barbara.

American Memory. Materials related to American history that has been digitized by the Library of Congress.

API (Application Programming Interface). A computer software program that facilitates interaction between different software programs located in different places.

Applet. A small computer program that can be transmitted to a client computer, cell phone or personal digital assistant (PDA). Also, sometimes called an App.

Archival Information Package (AIP). The internal representation of an object into a digital repository, including all data generated upon ingest (e.g., descriptive metadata) needed to manage and preserve it.

Archive. Collection of related materials and services that emphasize the long-term preservation of materials and their contents.

Art and Architecture Thesaurus. A thesaurus for fine art, decorative art, material culture, and architecture created by the J. Paul Getty Trust.

Artifact. A physical object in a library, archive or museum.

Authentication. A process to validate a user, a computer, or some digital object to ensure that it is what it claims to be.

Authorization. Permission given to a client computer or user to access specific information, and carry out approved actions.

Bandwidth. The amount of data that may be transmitted through a network in a fixed period of time.

Behaviors Metadata. Metadata used to associate executable behaviors with content in the METS object. A behavior section has an interface definition element that represents an abstract definition of the set of behaviors represented by a particular behavior section. A behavior section also has a behavior mechanism, which is a module of executable code that implement and runs the behaviors defined abstractly by the interface definition.

Bit-depth. The number of bits used to express the color of a pixel. Each pixel can contain up to three channels for color, each of which can be expressed in up to 8 bits.

Bluetooth. A wireless communication protocol providing short-range links between electronic devices.

Born Digital. An object is created in digital format and no analog "hard copy" counterpart exists.

Browser. A general-purpose user interface software, typically used with the World Wide Web or Web. Often times called a Web browser.

California Digital Library. A digital library that serves the nine campuses of the University of California.

Catalog. A collection of bibliographic records created according to a specified set of rules.

CIDOC CRM (CIDOC Conceptual Reference Model). Developed by the International Council of Museums (ICM), CIDOC refers to the ICM's International Committee for Documentation. The CIDOC CRM domain model covers description, object management and preservation.

Classification. A set of library materials organized by a hierarchy of subject categories. One example of a classification system is the Library of Congress Subject Headings (LCSH).

CMYK. A color model composed of four colors – cyan, magenta, yellow and black used for offset printing.

Complex Digital Object. Includes two or more content files (and their format variants or derivatives) and corresponding metadata. The content files are related as parts of a whole and are sequenced logically, such as pages.

Component. Content file or a metadata package that is part of a digital object.

Compression. The reduction in the size of digital materials by removing redundancy or by approximation. *Lossless* compression can be reversed; *lossy* compression cannot be reversed since information is lost due to approximation.

Content File. A file that is either born digitally or produced using various kinds of capture application software. Audio, image, text, and video are the basic kinds of content files.

Conversion. Transformation of information from one medium to another. For example, converting paper to digital form.

Crowdsourcing. An open call to an undefined group of people to perform tasks, solve problems, and contribute fresh ideas.

CSS (Cascading Style Sheets). A system of style sheets for use with HTML.

Data Content Standard. Rules for determining and formulating data values within metadata elements. Examples include the Anglo-American Cataloging Rules (AACR), Cataloging Cultural Objects (CCO), Describing

Archives: a Content Standard (DACS), and Graphic Materials (GIHC).

Data Interchange Standard. Used to define the encoding, storage, transmission, and interchange of data values represented within a data structure standard. Examples include the Dublin Core RDF/XML, MODS, and MARC21 formats.

Data Set. Any data organized in a defined set such as lists, tables, and databases.

Data Structure Standard. Standards that define metadata elements. Examples of data structure standards include Dublin Core, MODS, and MARC21.

Data type. Structural metadata associated with digital data that indicates the digital format or the application used to process the data.

DCMI (Dublin Core Metadata Initiative). Transformed the original fifteen-metadata elements into an extensible and flexible RDA-compliant set of metadata.

Descriptive Metadata. Metadata used for the discovery and interpretation of the digital object. Descriptive metadata may be referred to indirectly by pointing from the digital wrapper to a metadata object, a MARC record, or an EAD instance located elsewhere. Or, descriptive metadata may be embedded in the appropriate section of the digital wrapper.

Dewey Decimal Classification. A classification scheme for library materials that uses a numeric code to indicate subject areas.

Digital Library Federation (DLF). A consortium of libraries and related agencies that are pioneering the use of digital technologies to extend their collections and services. The DLF became a part of the Council on Library and Information Resources in June 2010.

Digital Master. A digital object that most closely retains the significant attributes of the original. Typically the highest quality digital object of the original.

Digital Object. An item as stored in a digital library, consisting of data, metadata, and an identifier.

Digital Object Identifier (DOI). An identifier used by publishers to uniquely identify materials published electronically.

Digital Preservation. The set of managed activities necessary for ensuring the long-term retention and usability of digital objects.

Digital Wrapper. A structured text file that binds digital object content files and their associated metadata together and that specifies the logical relationship of the content files. METS is an emerging, XML-based international standard for wrapping digital library materials. All of the content files and corresponding metadata may be embedded in the digital wrapper and stored with the wrapper. This is called physical wrapping or embedding. Or, the content files and metadata may be stored independently of the wrapper and referred to by file pointers from within the wrapper. This is called logical wrapping or referencing. A digital object may partake of both kinds of wrapping.

D-Lib Magazine. A monthly online publication that discussed digital libraries research and innovation.

Document Type Definition (DTD). A common way of defining the structure, elements, and attributes that is available for use in a SGML or XML document that complies with the DTD.

Dublin Core. A simple set of metadata elements used in digital libraries, primarily to describe digital objects and for collection management, and for the exchange of metadata.

EAD. Encoded Archival Description.

Electronic journal. An online publication that is organized similar to a traditional printed journal. The electronic journal may be an online version of the printed journal or a journal that is only published in an online format.

Element. A discrete component of metadata, or a discrete component of a data structure defined by a DTD or schema (often represented through markup in the form of a tag).

Encoded Archival Description (EAD). Document Type Definition that assists in the creation of electronic finding aids. An EAD can be used to represent complete archival structures, including hierarchies and associations.

Fair use. A concept in copyright law that allows limited use of copyright material for scholarship or review without requiring permission from the rights holders.

Finding Aid. A guide or inventory to a collection held in an archive, museum, library, or historical society. It provides a detailed description of a collection, its intellectual organization and, at varying levels of analysis, of individual items in the collection.

FRBR (Functional Requirements for Bibliographic Records). A cataloging standard that replaces the Anglo-American Cataloging Rules (AACR2). FRBR is a conceptual entity-relationship model developed by the International Federation of Library Associations (IFLA) that relates users tasks of retrieval from a user's perspective.

Genre. The class or category of an object when considered as an intellectual work.
Geospatial information. Information that is referenced by a geographic location.

GIF (Graphics Interchange Format). A format for storing compressed images.

GIS (Geographic Information System). A system that integrates, stores, edits, analyzes, shares, and displays geographic information.

Harvest. The process by which software can collect and store metadata packages from remote locations that describe information resources available at those locations.

Home page. The introductory page to a collection of information on the Web.

HTML (Hypertext Markup Language). A simple markup and formatting language for text, with links to other objects, used with the Web.

HTTP (Hypertext Transfer Protocol). The basic protocol for the Web used for communication between browsers and Web sites.

Hyperlink. A network link from one item in a digital library or Web site to another.

Hypertext. A non-linear system of information browsing and retrieval that contains associated links to other related content and documents.

Information discovery. General term covering all strategies and methods of finding information in a digital library.

Information retrieval. Searching a body of information for objects that match a search query.

Ingest. The process by which a digital object or metadata package is absorbed by a different system than the one that produced it.

IP (Internet Protocol). The communications standard for relaying small packets of data across the Internet.

Java. A software programming language developed by Sun Microsystems.

JavaScript. A scripting language used to embed executable instructions in a Web page.

JPEG (Joint Photographic Experts Group). A format for storing compressed images.

Link. A URL that references resources integral to the digital object.

LOCKSS (Lots of Copies Keeps Stuff Safe). A Internet-based preservation initiative.

Los Alamos E-Print Archives. An open-access Web site for rapid distribution of research papers pertaining to physics and related disciplines.

Lossless. A file compression technique in which all information in the original is recoverable yet files can be compressed to reduce file size.

Lossy. A file compression technique in which lost information of the original is not recoverable.

LZW. Lempel-Ziv-Welch (LZW) is a universal lossless data compression algorithm.

MARC (Machine-Readable Cataloging). A format used by libraries to store and exchange bibliographic information.

Markup language. Codes embedded in a document that describes its structure and/or its format.

Memex. A concept for an online library suggested by Vannevar Bush in 1945.

Metadata. Data about other data, typically divided into *descriptive* metadata such as bibliographic information, *structural* metadata about formats and structures, and *administrative* metadata, which is used to manage information.

Metadata harvest. The harvest of existing metadata records from resource repositories, such as through OAI, to gather metadata for query results or index creation.

METS (Metadata Encoding and Transmission Standard). METS, a NISO standard, is expressed in XML that provides a means to convey the metadata necessary for the management of digital objects and the exchange of such objects between repositories.

Migration. The transfer of digital objects from one hardware or software configuration to another, or from one generation of computer technology to a subsequent generation. The purpose of migration is to preserve the integrity of digital objects; and to retain the ability for clients to retrieve, display, and use them in the face of constantly changing technology.

MPEG (Moving Picture Expert Group). A family of formats for compressing and storing digitized video and sound.

MODS (Metadata Object Description Schema). MODS is an XML schema that includes a subset of MARC fields and uses language-based tags rather than numeric ones.

NISO. National Information Standards Organization.

NSF (National Science Foundation). A U.S. government agency that supports science and engineering research, including research for digital libraries.

OAI (Open Archives Initiative). The Open Archives Initiative develops and promotes interoperability standards that aim to facilitate the efficient dissemination of content.

Object. A digital object is a digital representation of an analog item.

Open Archival Information System (OAIS). A conceptual framework for an archival system dedicated to preserving and maintaining access to digital information over the long term.

OAI-PMH (Open Archives Initiative Protocol for Metadata Harvesting). OAI-PMH provides an application-independent interoperability framework based on *metadata harvesting.*

OCLC (Online Computer Library Center). A not-for-profit organization that provides a range of services to libraries that is headquartered in Dublin, Ohio.

OCR (Optical Character Recognition). Automatic conversion of text from a digitized image to computer text.

ONIX (Online Information eXchange). The ONIX for Books Product Information Message is the international standard for representing and communicating book industry product information in electronic form. Several organizations have developed mappings from ONIX to MARC, the most widely-used format for data exchange among libraries.

OPAC (Online Public Access Catalog). An online library catalog.

Open access. Resources that are openly available to users with no need for authentication or payment.

OWL (Web Ontology Language). Allows for the expression of vocabularies and relationships between terms in a way that facilities the development of computer applications that use the vocabularies.

PDF (Portable Document Format). A page description language to store and display images of pages.

Persistent Identifier. An identifier that will stay with a digital object despite any moves to a different storage location, manipulation of the datastream and so forth.

Pixel. A pixel or picture element is the smallest addressable screen element.

Policy. Rule established by a digital library manager to control access to materials.

Portal. A Web site that offers services such as directories, searching, news, and links to related Web sites.

Protocol. A set of rules that describe the sequence of messages sent across a network, specifying the syntax and semantics.

Public Domain. Material that is available to the public since it is out of copyright or unable to be copyrighted in the first place, e.g., a government publication.

PURL (Persistent URL). A method of providing persistent identifiers using standard Web protocols.

Query. A search request used in information retrieval to find objects or records that match the request.

RDA (Resource Description and Access). Designed for the digital world and an expanding universe of metadata users, RDA is the unified cataloging standard—an evolution of the cataloging principles from AACR2, with rules carried over or adapted to the RDA model.

RDF (Resource Description Framework). A method for specifying the syntax of metadata, used to exchange data.

Replication. Make copies of digital material for backup, reliability, improved performance or preservation.

Resolution. The number of pixels (in both height and width) making up a digital image. The higher the resolution, the greater its visual definition and density. Resolution is often referred to as dots per inch (dpi).

RFID (Radio Frequency Identification). Uses a tag for the purpose of identification and tracking using radio waves.

RGB. A color model based on the three primary colors of red, green and blue.

Rights Management Administrative Metadata. Administrative metadata that indicates the copyrights, user restrictions, and license agreements that might constrain the end-use of the content files.

Saturation. The strength of purity of a color.

Scanning. Method of conversion in which a physical object, for example a printed page, is represented by a digital grid of pixels.

Schema. A common way of defining the structure, elements, and attributes that are available for use in a XML document that complies to the schema.

SGML (Standard Generalized Markup Language). A system for creating markup languages that represent the structure of a document. SGML is an international standard (ISO 8879).

SICI (Serial Item and Contribution Identifier). A unique identifier for an issue of a serial or an article contained within a serial.

SKOS (Simple Knowledge Organization System). A standard way to represent organized data such as thesauri, classification schemes, and subject heading schemes.

Source Administrative Metadata. Administrative metadata for describing the source from which the digital content files were produced. Sometimes this will be the original material; other times it will be an intermediary such as a photographic slide, or another digital content file.

Structural type. Metadata that indicates the structural category of a digital object.

Structural Metadata. Metadata used to indicate the logical or physical relationship of the content files comprising the complex digital object, e.g., the sequence of pages for a group of images of a diary or of detailed images of a larger image. The structural metadata specifies a coherent presentation of the digital content and its relevant associated metadata.

Style sheet. A set of rules that indicates how markup in a document translates into the appearance of the document when displayed.

Tag. A special string of characters embedded in marked-up text to indicate the structure or format.

Tagging. Words used by people to describe a Web site, picture, blog posting and so forth. Tags used by people are often disorganized and redundant.

Technical Metadata. Administrative metadata that describes the technical attributes of the digital file.

Text Encoding Initiative (TEI). An initiative that publishes Document Type Definitions catering to a wide range of academic electronic text projects. Books, manuscripts, and other kinds of literary and linguistic texts for online research and teaching that are available electronically are encoded in TEI.

Thumbnail. A small version of an image that acts as a link to a larger version of the same image.

TIFF (Tagged Image File Format). A file format for digital images.

Unicode. An international standard that uses a 16-bit computer code to represent the characters used in most of the world's written scripts.

URI (Uniform Resource Identifier). A string of characters used to identify a name or resource on the Internet.

URL (Uniform Resource Locator). A reference to a resource on the internet specifying a protocol, a computer (server), domain name, or file on a computer.

W3C (World Wide Web Consortium). An international community that develops standards to ensure the long-term growth of the Web.

Web crawler. A Web indexing program that builds an index by following every hyperlink from Web page to Web page.

WiFi. The term WiFi suggests *Wireless Fidelity* but is actually a brand name for the IEEE 802.11 standards that provides wireless communications.

World Wide Web (Web). An interlinked set of information sources on the Internet.

Work. The underlying intellectual abstraction behind some material in a digital library.

XML (eXtensible Markup Language). A simplified version of SGML intended for use with online information.

Z39.50. A standard protocol that allows a computer to retrieve information, mainly bibliographic information, from other computers.

270

References

AAP –Association of American Publishers. *AAP Reports Book Sales Estimated at $23.9 Billion in 2009.* News Release. April 7, 2010. Available at www.publishers.org

Edward Abbey Available at http://thinkexist.com/search/searchquotation.asp?search=glut+of+information&q

Abrizah Abdullah and A.N. Zainab. The Digital Library as an Enterprise: The Zachman Approach. *The Electronic Library*, 26 (4), 2008, 446-467.

Alan Aldrich. Universities and Libraries Move to the Mobile Web. *Educause Quarterly*, 33 (2), 2010. Available at http://www.educause.edu/EDUCAUSE+Quarterly/EDUCAUSEQuarterlyMagazineVolum/UniversitiesandLibrariesMoveto/206531

Mehdi Alipour-Hafezi, Abbas Horri, Ali Shiri, and Amir Ghaebi. Interoperability Models in Digital Libraries: An Overview. *The Electronic Library*, 28 (3), 2010, 438-452.

Chris Anderson and Michael Wolff. The Web Is Dead. Long Live the Internet. *Wired*, September 2010, 122-127. Available at http://www.wired.com/magazine/2010/08/ff_webrip/

Janna Anderson and Lee Rainie. *The Future of Cloud Computing.* Washington, DC: Pew Research Center Internet & American Life Project, June 2010. Available at http://pewresearch.org/pubs/1623/future-cloud-computing-technology-experts

William Arms. Key Concepts in the Architecture of the Digital Library. *D-Lib Magazine,* 1 (1), July 1995. Available at http://www.dlib.org/dlib/July95/07arms.html

William Arms, Naomi Dushay, Dave Fulker and Carl Lagoze. A Case Study in Metadata Harvesting: The NSDL. *Library HiTech*, 21 (2), 2003, 228-237.

David Bawden and Ian Rowlands. Digital Libraries: Assumptions and Concepts. *Libri*, 49 (4), 1999, 181-191. Available at http://www.librijournal.org/pdf/1999-4pp181-191.pdf

David Bearman. Digital Libraries. *The Annual Review of Information Science and Technology*, 41 (1), 2007, 223-272.

Roger Bohn and James Short. *How Much Information? 2009 Report on American Consumers*. San Diego: University of California San Diego, 2009. Available at http://hmi.ucsd.edu/pdf/HMI_2009_ConsumerReport_Dec9_20 09.pdf

Daniel Boorstein. Available at http://thinkexist.com/quotation/technology_is_so_much_fun_ but_we_can_drown_in_our/203046.html

Christine L. Borgman. What are Digital Libraries? Competing Visions. *Information Processing and Management*, 35 (3), 1999, 227-243.

Marshall Breeding. Maximizing the Impact of Digital Collections. *Computers in Libraries,* April 2009, 22-24. Available at http://www.librarytechnology.org/ltg-displaytext.pl?RC=13931

British Library. *British Library Predicts 'Switch to Digital by 2020.'* News Release, June 29, 2005. Available at www.bl.uk
Steven Buchanan and Adeola Salako. Evaluating the Usability and Usefulness of a Digital Library. *Library Review*, 58 (9), 2009, 638-651.

272

Jerry D. Campbell. Changing a Cultural Icon: The Academic Library as a Virtual Destination. *Educause Review*, 41 (1) January/February 2006, 16-31. Available at http://net.educause.edu/ir/library/pdf/erm0610.pdf

Nicholas Carr. *The Big Switch: Rewiring the World, from Edison to Google.* New York: Norton & Company, 2008.

Cameron Chapman. *10 Usability Tips Based on Research Studies.* September 15, 2010. Available at http://sixrevisions.com/usabilityaccessibility/10-usability-tips-based-on-research-studies/

Xiaotian Chen. MetaLib, WebFeat, and Google: The Strengths and Limitations of Federated Search Engines Compared with Google. *Online Information Review*, 30 (4), 2006, 413-427.

Youngok Choi and Edie Rasmussen. What Qualifications and Skills are Important for Digital Librarian Positions in Academic Libraries? A Job Advertisement Analysis. *The Journal of Academic Librarianship*, 35 (5), September 2009, 457-467.

Timothy Cole. Creating a Framework of Guidance for Building Good Digital Collections. *FirstMonday*, 7 (5/6), May 2002. Available at http://firstmonday.org/htbin/cgiwrap/bin/ojs/index.php/fm/article/view/955/876

Council on Library and Information Resources. *No Brief Candle: Reconceiving Research Libraries for the 21st Century.* CLIR publication No. 142. Washington, DC: Council on Library and Information Resources, 2008. Available at http://www.clir.org/pubs/reports/pub142/pub142.pdf

Alan Dawson. *Revising Digital Library Content in Response to User Requests.* 2006. Available at http://eprints.rclis.org/bitstream/10760/13496/1/AD3.doc.pdf

Loren Dempsey. *The Sound of Words: Amazoogle and Googlezon.* Weblog of January 29, 2005. Available at http://orweblog.oclc.org/archives/000562.html

DLF (Digital Library Federation). *A Working Definition of the Digital Library.* 1998. Available at http://www.diglib.org/about/dldefinition.htm

Ross Duncan. Ebooks and Beyond: The Challenge for Public Libraries. *Aplis,* 23 (2), June 2010, 44- 55.

Ricky Erway. Defining "Born Digital." Dublin, OH: OCLC, November 2010. Available at http://www.oclc.org/research/activities/hiddencollections/born digital.pdf

Philip Evans and Thomas Wurster. *Blown to Bits : How the New Economics of Information Transforms Strategy.* Boston: Harvard Business School Press, 1997.

Geoffrey Fowler and Marie Baca. The ABCs of E-Reading. *The Wall Street Journal (Online),* August 24, 2010. Available at http://online.wsj.com/article/SB1000142405274870384660457 5448093175758872.html

Edward A. Fox and Shalini R. Urs. Digital Libraries. *Annual Review of Information Science & Technology,* 36, 2002, 502-589.

Jonathan Furner. User Tagging of Library Resources: Toward a Framework for System Evaluation. *International Cataloguing and Bibliographic Control,* 37 (3), July/September 2008, 47-51.

Peter Gerstberger and Thomas Allen. *Criteria for Selection of an Information Source.* Working Paper #284-67. Cambridge, MA: Alfred P. Sloan School Of Management, Massachusetts Institute Of Technology, September 1967. 24 pages.

Carol Jean Godby. *Mapping ONIX to MARC.* Dublin, OH: OCLC, 2010. Available at http://www.oclc.org/research/publications/library/2010/2010-14.pdf

Anthony Grafton . Apocalypse in the stacks? The research library in the age of Google. *Daedalus,* 138 (1), Winter 2009, 87-98.

Mark Greene and Dennis Meissner. More Product, Less Product: Revamping Traditional Archival Processing. *The American Archivist,* 68 (2), 2005, 208-263. Available at http://archivists.metapress.com/content/c741823776k65863/fulltext.pdf

Gretchen Gueguen & Ann Hanlon. A Collaborative Workflow for the Digitization of Unique Materials. *The Journal of Academic Librarianship,* 35 (5), September 2009, 468-474.

Katie Hafner. History, Digitized (and Abridged). Your Money. *The New York Times* Business section, March 11, 2007. Available at http://query.nytimes.com/gst/fullpage.html?res=9500E5DC1331F932A25750C0A9619C8B63

Yan Han. On the Clouds: A New Way of Computing. *Information Technology and Libraries,* June 2010, 87-92. Available at http://www.ala.org/ala/mgrps/divs/lita/ital/292010/2902jun/han_pdf.cfm

Dan Hazen. Rethinking Research Library Collections: A Policy Framework for Straitened Times and Beyond. *Library Resources & Technical Services,* 54 (2), April 2010, 115-21.

Allison J. Head and Michael B. Eisenberg. *Truth Be Told: How College Students Evaluate and Use Information in the Digital Age.* Seattle: The Information School, University of Washington, November 1, 2010. Available at http://projectinfolit.org/pdfs/PIL_Fall2010_Survey_FullReport1.pdf

Allison J. Head and Michael B. Eisenberg. *Finding Context: What Today's College Students Say About Conducting Research in the Digital Age.* Seattle: The Information School, University of Washington, February 4, 2009. Available at http://projectinfolit.org/pdfs/PIL_ProgressReport_2_2009.pdf

Peter Hernon, Rosita Hopper, Michael R. Leach, Laura L. Saunders, and Jane Zhang. E-Book use by Students: Undergraduates in Economics, Literature, and Nursing. *The Journal of Academic Librarianship*, 33, 2007, 3-13.

Rose Holley. Tagging Full Text Searchable Articles: An Overview of Social Tagging Activity in Historic Australian Newspapers August 2008 – August 2009. *D-Lib Magazine*, 16 (1/2), January/February 2010. Available at http://www.dlib.org/dlib/january10/holley/01holley.html

Rose Holley. Crowdsourcing: How and Why Should Libraries Do It? *D-Lib Magazine*, 16 (3/4), March/April 2010. Available at http://www.dlib.org/dlib/march10/holley/03holley.html

ISO 13407: Human-Centered Design Processes for Interactive Systems. Geneva: International Organization for Standardization, 1999.

JISC. *The Impact of Search Engine Optimization on Organizations' Websites.* Ottawa: Canadian Heritage Information Network, November 2009.

Richard Katz. Scholars, Scholarship, and the Scholarly Enterprise in the Digital Age. *EDUCAUSE Review*, 45 (2), March/April 2010, 44-56. Available at http://www.educause.edu/EDUCAUSE+Review/EDUCAUSERevie wMagazineVolume45/ScholarsScholarshipandtheSchol/202341

Alan Kay. Available at http://www.smalltalk.org/alankay.html

Kevin Kelly. Scan This Book! *The New York Times Magazine*, May 14, 2006, 42-51. Available at http://www.nytimes.com/2006/05/14/magazine/14publishing. html

Steve Kolowich. Libraries of the Future. *Inside Higher Ed*, September 24, 2009. Available at http://www.insidehighered.com/news/2009/09/24/libraries

Brian Lavoie, Lynn Silipigni Connaway, and Lorcan Dempsey. Anatomy of Aggregate Collections: The Example of Google Print for Libraries. *D-Lib Magazine*, 11 (9), September 2005.

Library of Congress (2011). Available at http://www.digitalpreservation.gov/education/index.html

Library of Congress. Guidelines for Electronic Preservation of Visual Materials. Washington, DC: Library of Congress, October 18, 2006. Available at http://www.loc.gov/preserv/guide/guid_dig.html

J.C.R. Licklider. *Libraries of the Future*. Cambridge, MA: The MIT Press, 1965.

Chern Li Liew. Digital Library Research 1997 – 2007: Organisational and People Issues. *Journal of Documentation*, 65 (2), 2009, 245-266.

David W. Lewis. What If Libraries Are Artifact-Bound Institutions? *Information Technology & Libraries*, 17 (4), December 1998, 191-97. Available at https://scholarworks.iupui.edu/bitstream/handle/1805/434/Lewis%2BDW%2B-%2BWhat%2Bif%2BLibrar.pdf?sequence=6

John Lombardi. Academic Libraries in a Digital Age. *D-Lib Magazine*, 6 (10), October 2000. Available at http://www.dlib.org/dlib/october00/lombardi/10lombardi.html

Laurie Lopatin. Library Digitization Projects, Issues and Guidelines: A Survey of the Literature. *Library HiTech*, 24 (2), 2006, 273-289.

Mark Ludwig and Margaret Wells. Is the BISON Catalog Going the Way of Its Namesake? *Library Journal*, 133 (11), June 15, 2008, 30-2. Available at http://www.libraryjournal.com/article/CA6566451.html

Peter Lyman and Hal Varian. *How Much Information?* Berkeley: University of California, 1999. Available at http://www2.sims.berkeley.edu/research/projects/how-much-info/summary.html

Peter Lyman and Hal Varian. *How Much Information?* 2003 Berkeley: University of California, 2003. Available at http://chnm.gmu.edu/digitalhistory/links/pdf/preserving/8_5a.pdf

Alexis Madrigal. Inside the Google Books Algorithm. *The Atlantic*, November 1, 2010. Available at http://www.theatlantic.com/technology/archive/2010/11/inside-the-google-books-algorithm/65422/

278

Stephann Makri, Ann Blandford, Jeremy Gow, Jon Rimmer and Claire Warwick and George Buchanan. A Library or Just Another Information Resource? A Case Study of Users' Mental Models of Traditional and Digital Libraries. *Journal of the American Society for Information Science and Technology*, 58 (3), 2007, 433-445.

Constance Malpas. Cloud Sourcing Research Collections. PowerPoint presentation at the RLG Partnership Meeting, June 2010. Available at www.oclc.org/**research**/events/20100609h.pptx

Thomas Mann's *Library Research Models: A Guide to Classification, Cataloging, and Computers* New York: Oxford University Press, 1993.

Gary Marchionini, C Plaisant and A Komlodi. The People in Digital Libraries: Multifaceted Approaches to assessing Needs and Impacts, in Ann Bishop, Nancy Van House, and Barbara Buttenfield (Eds.). *Digital Library Use: Social Practice in Design and Evaluation.* Cambridge, MA: MIT Press, 2003.

Joseph R. Matthews. *The Customer-Focused Library: Re-inventing the Public Library From the Outside In.* Westport, CN: Libraries Unlimited, 2009.

Joseph R. Matthews. *The Evaluation and Measurement of Library Services.* Westport, CN: Libraries Unlimited, 2007. Krystyna Matusiak. Towards User-Centered Indexing in Digital Image Collections. *OCLC Systems & Services*, 22 (4), 2006, 283-298.

John Maxymut. 13 Ways of Looking at Googlebrary. *The Bottom Line*, 18 (4), 2005, 197-201.

Kitty McClanahan, Lei Wu, Carol Tenopir and Donald King. Embracing change: Perceptions of e-journal by University Faculty Members. *Learned Publishing*, 23 (3), July 2010, 209-223. Available at http://www.inforum.cz/pdf/2009/tenopir-carol-eng.pdf

Marshall McLuhan. The Best of Ideas, *CBC Radio*, 1967. Available at http://faculty.uml.edu/sgallagher/marshall_mcluhan.htm

Peter Michel. Digitizing Special Collections: To Boldly Go Where We've Been Before. *Library HiTech*, 23 (3), 2005, 379-395.

Clement Mok. *Designing Business: Multiple Media, Multiple Disciplines*. London: Hayden Books, 1996.

Peter Morville. *Ambient Findability*. Sebastopol, CA: O'Reilly, 2005.

David Nicholas, Paul Huntington and Jamali Hamid. The Information seeking Behavior of the Users of Digital Scholarly Journals. *Information Processing and Management*, 42 (5), September 2006, 1345-65.

Jakob Nielsen. *Multimedia and Hypertext: The Internet and Beyond*. Boston: Academic Press, 1995, 281.

NINCH – National Initiative for a Networked Cultural Heritage. *The NINCH Guide to Good Practice in the Digital Representation and Management of Cultural Heritage Materials*. Glasgow, Scotland: The University of Glasgow, 2003. Available at http://www.ninch.org/guide.pdf

NISO. *A Framework of Guidance for Building Good Digital Collections*. Washington, DC: NISO Framework Working Group, December 2007. Available at http://framework.niso.org/

Megan Oakleaf. *The Value of Academic Libraries: A Comprehensive Research Review and Report.* Chicago: Association of College and Research Libraries, 2010. Available at http://www.acrl.ala.org/value/

OCLC. *Environmental Scan: Pattern Recognition.* Dublin, OH: OCLC Online Computer Library Center, 2003. Available at http://www.oclc.org/reports/escan/

OCLC. *Perceptions of Libraries and Information Resources.* Dublin, OH: OCLC Online Computer Library Center, 2005. Available at http://www.oclc.org/reports/2005perceptions.htm

OCLC. College Students' *Perceptions of Libraries and Information Resources.* Dublin, OH: OCLC Online Computer Library Center, 2006. Available at http://www.oclc.org/reports/pdfs/studentperceptions.pdf

OCLC. Well-Intentioned Practice for Putting Digitized Collections of Unpublished Materials Online. Dublin, OH: OCLC Online Computer Library Center, 2010. Available at http://www.oclc.org/research/activities/rights

William Paisley. Predicting Library Circulation from Community Characteristics. *Public Opinion Quarterly,* 29 (1), Spring 1965, 39-53.

Marc Parry. After Losing Users in Catalog, Libraries Find Better Search Software. *The Chronicle for Higher Education,* 56 (6), September 28, 2009, A13. Available at http://chronicle.com/article/After-Losing-Users-in/48588/

Norman Paskin. Digital Object Identifier (DOI) System. *Encyclopedia of Library and Information Sciences,* Third Edition. 2010. Available at http://www.doi.org/overview/DOI-ELIS-Paskin.pdf

Pew Research Center Internet Project. *The Future of Cloud Computing*. Washington, DC: Pew Research Center Internet Project, 2010. Available at http://pewinternet.org/Reports/2010/The-future-of-cloud-computing.aspx

Pew Research Center Internet Project. The Internet Goes to College. Washington, DC: Pew Research Center Internet Project, 2002. Available at http://www.pewinternet.org/~/media/Files/Reports/2002/PIP_College_Report.pdf.pdf

Sue Polanka. *No shelf Required: E-Books in Libraries*. Chicago: ALA, 2011.

Jeffrey Pomerantz and Gary Marchionini. The Digital Library as Place. *Journal of Documentation*, 63 (4), 2007, 505-533.

Herbert Poole. *Theories of the Middle Range*. New York: Ablex, 1985.

Primary Research Group. *Survey of Library & Museum Digitization Projects 2011 Edition*. New York: Primary Research Group, 2010.
Shiyali Ranganathan. *The Five Laws of Library Science*. Madras, India: Madras Library Association, 1931. Available at http://www.cro.sanita.fvg.it/reposCRO/Biblioteca/5_leggi_ranganathan.pdf

Oya Rieger. Projects to Programs: Developing a Digital Preservation Policy, in *Moving Theory into Practice: Digital Imaging for Libraries and Archives*. Anne Kenney and Oya Rieger (Eds.). Mountain View, CA: Research Libraries Group, 2000, 135-152.

RIN – Research Information Network. *Ejournals: Their Use, Value, and Impact*. London: RIN, 2009. Available at www.ucl.ac.uk

RIN – Research Information Network. Researchers' Use of Academic Libraries and Their Services. London: RIN, 2007. Available at http://www.rin.ac.uk/our-work/using-and-accessing-information-resources/researchers-use-academic-libraries-and-their-serv

RLG. RLG Guidelines for Preparing a Request for Proposal for Digital Imaging Services. May 1998. Available at http://www.oclc.org/research/activities/past/rlg/digimgtools/RFPGuidelines.pdf

Victor Rosenberg. Factors Affecting the Preferences of Industrial Personnel for Information Gathering Methods. *Information Storage and Retrieval*, 3, 1967, 119-27.

Ian Rowlands and David Bawden. Building the Digital Library on Solid Research Foundations. *Aslib Proceedings*, 51 (8), September 1999, 275-282.

Ian Rowlands, David Nichols, Peter Williams, Paul Huntington, Maggie Fieldhouse, Barrie Gunter, Richard Withey, Hamid Jamali, Tom Dobrowolski, and Carol Tenopir. The Google Generation: The Information Behaviour of the Researcher of the Future. *Aslib Proceedings*, 60 (4), 2008, 290-310.

Beth St. Jean, Soo young Rieh, Elizabeth Yakel, and Karen Markey. Unheard Voices: Institutional Repository End-Users. College & Research Libraries, January 2011, 21-42.

John Salasin and Toby Cedar. Person-to-Person Communication in an Applied Research/Service Delivery Setting. *Journal of the American Society for Information Science*, March 1985, 36 (2), 103-115.

Dorothea Salo. Innkeeper at the Roach Motel. *Library Trends*, 57 (2), Fall 2008, 98. Available at https://www.ideals.illinois.edu/bitstream/handle/2142/10678/salo.pdf?sequence=2

Roger C. Schonfeld and Ross Housewright. *Faculty Survey 2009: Key Strategic Insights for Libraries, Publishers, and Societies.* April 7, 2010. Available at http://www.ithaka.org/ithaka-s-r/research/faculty-surveys-2000-2009/Faculty%20Study%202009.pdf

Candy Schwartz. Thesauri and Facets and Tags, Oh My! A Look at Three Decades in Subject Analysis. *Library Trends*, 56 (4), Spring 2008, 830-842. Available at https://www.ideals.illinois.edu/handle/2142/9495

Patricia Serotkin, Patricia Fitzgerald and Sandra Balough. If We Build It, Will They Come? Electronic Journals Acceptance and Usage Patterns. *portal: Libraries and the Academy*, 5 (4), October 2005, 497-512.

Lisa Spiro and Geneva Henry. Can a New Research Library Be All-Digital? In *The Idea of Order: Transforming Research Collections for 21st Century Scholarship*. CLIR Publication No. 147. Washington, DC: The Council on Library and Information Resources, 2010. Available at http://www.clir.org/pubs/reports/pub147/pub147.pdf

Harry Stewart. Quote from the Digitization 101 blog by Jill Hurst –Wahl. Available at http://hurstassociates.blogspot.com/2010/12/quote-about-emerging-theme-in-digital.html

Simon Tanner, Trevor Munoz and Pich Hemy Ros. Measuring Mass Text Digitization Quality and Usefulness. *D-Lib Magazine*, 15 (7/8), July/August 2009.
Techcrunch 2009. Available at http://techcrunch.com/2009/03/29/the-wounded-us-newspaper-industry-lost-75-billion-in-advertising-revenues-last-year/

284

Roy Tennant. The Top Ten Things Library Administrators Should Know About Technology. *TechEssence.info blog*, September 12, 2009. Available at http://www.techessence.info/topten

Carol Tenopir, Donald King, Sheri Edwards and Lei Wu. Electronic Journals and Changes in Scholarly Article Seeking and Reading Patterns. *Aslib Proceedings: New Information Perspectives*, 61 (1), 2009, 5-32.

Carol Tenopir and Donald King. Perceptions of Value and Value Beyond Perceptions: Measuring the Quality and Value of Journal Article Readings. *Serials*, 20 (3), 2007, 199-207.

Giannis Tsakonas and Christos Papatheodorou. Exploring Usefulness and Usability in the Evaluation of Open Access Digital Libraries. *Information Processing and Management*, 44, 2008, 1234-1250.

Siva Vaidhyanathan. *The Googlization of Everything: (And Why We Should Worry)*. Berkeley: University of California Press, 2010.

Paul Valery. Available at http://thinkexist.com/quotation/books-have-the-same-enemies-as-people-fire/365681.html

Jason Vaughn. Web Scale Discovery: What and Why? *Library Technology Reports*, 47 (1), January 2011, 5-11.

Ben Vershbow. The Really Modern Library. *If:book blog*. October 8, 2007. Available at http://www.futureofthebook.org/blog/archives/2007/10/the_really_modern_library.html

Timothy Vollmer. *There's an App for That!* Washington, DC: ALA Office for Information Technology Policy, 2010. Available at http://www.ala.org/ala/aboutala/offices/oitp/publications/policybriefs/mobiledevices.pdf

Gay Walker, Jane Greenfield, John Fox, and Jeffrey Simonoff. The Yale Survey: A Large-Scale Study of Book Deterioration in the Yale University Library. *College & Research Libraries*, 46, 1985, 111-132.

Gary Wang and Zao Liu. Content-Based Information Retrieval and Digital Libraries. *Information Technology & Libraries*, 27 (1), March 2008, 41-47.

David Weinberger. *Everything is Miscellaneous.* New York: Holt, 2007.

Hong Iris Xie. Evaluation of Digital Libraries: Criteria and Problems from Users' Perspectives. *Library & Information Science Research*, 28, 2006, 433-452.

David Zax. National Digital Public Library Gets One Step Closer to Reality. *Fast Company*, October 7, 2010. Available at http://www.fastcompany.com/1693581/making-a-national-digital-public-library-a-reality

Yongli Zhou. Are Your Digital Documents Web Friendly? Making Scanned Documents Web Accessible. *Information Technology and Libraries*, September 2010, 151-160. Available at http://www.ala.org/ala/mgrps/divs/lita/ital/292010/2903sep/z hou_pdf.cfm

George Zipf. *Human Behavior and the Principle of Least Effort.* Cambridge, MA: Addison-Wesley, 1949.

Index

288

290

About the Author

Joe has provided consulting assistance to numerous academic, public and special libraries and local governments.

He was also an instructor at the School of Library Information Science (SLIS) at San Jose State University. Joe taught evaluation of library services, library information systems, strategic planning, management and research methods. He was selected as the SLIS Outstanding Scholar in 2008.

In addition to numerous articles, he is the author of *Library Assessment in Higher Education, The Customer-Focused Library, The Evaluation and Measurement of Library Services, Scorecards for Results, Strategic Planning and Management for Library Managers*, and *Measuring for Results* among other books.

Joe is an invited conference speaker and is active in the American Library Association. A dedicated grandfather, Joe resides in Carlsbad, CA.